SUCCESS IN
HILL
COUNTRY

SUCCESS IN HILL COUNTRY

by Amy Clark

An Approved Publication of The Napoleon Hill Foundation

MEDIA

MEDIA

Published 2019 by Gildan Media LLC
aka G&D Media
www.GandDmedia.com

Front Cover design by David Rheinhardt of Pyrographx

Interior design by Meghan Day Healey of Story Horse, LLC

Library of Congress Cataloging-in-Publication Data is available upon request

ISBN: 978-1-7225-0105-1

10 9 8 7 6 5 4 3 2 1

For Bryan, Landon and Riley

CONTENTS

ACKNOWLEDGMENTS

I would like to thank Don Green and the Napoleon Hill Foundation for giving me the opportunity to turn this idea into a book. I also extend my appreciation to the generous people in these chapters who shared their time, stories and wisdom for this project.

Special thanks goes to Sharon Ewing, Director of the Southwest Virginia Museum Historical State Park, who provided valuable research on some of the people profiled in these pages.

Finally, I am infinitely grateful to my family for their unconditional faith and support and to my writing family, who, like me, are from these hallowed hills.

FOREWORD

Don M. Green,
Executive Director
Napoleon Hill Foundation

Amy Clark has been a longtime friend of the Napoleon Hill Foundation. She is always willing to share her skills with others.

Now, Clark has used her talents to interview and write *Success in Hill Country*, a collection of oral histories that combats the stereotyped image of people of the mountains, the same mountains where Napoleon Hill grew up and left to study the successful people of his time. Hill later became the best-selling motivational writer of all time. Clark has used her educational background and experience to interview and write of super achievers who have been successful and have given back to their communities.

Clark is a brilliant, easy to read author, and her stories will inspire you. The people she has written about will dispel any myths about mountain people as lazy or lacking ambition—an image that was created by television and movies. While the media meant to entertain, it left an impression with the public that simply is not true.

The Appalachian region has not only produced many wealthy individuals but also famous authors, athletes, women and men of business, educators, and other professionals who rank among the elite in our society. Clark's interviews and commentary leave the reader to appreciate the fact that dreams can come true—not just for the people in this book, but for readers who are also inspired to make their dreams come true.

As the executive director of the Napoleon Hill Foundation, I highly commend Clark on her work. After reading the book, I suggest you visit the authors section of *Applying Hill's Principles in Your Own Life* and the appendix with *Questions to Inspire Your Success Story*. Remember: the worth of any self help book is determined by the ways you can apply what you have learned after reading it.

AUTHOR'S NOTE

When Don Green and I sat down to discuss this book idea several years ago, I was elated because it would give me the opportunity to say what so many of us in Appalachia believe: that we are America's best-kept secret. *How* to write such a book was not as clear but then we realized that Napoleon Hill had the perfect design in *Think and Grow Rich*: interview successful people to determine how they accomplished their goals.

I expected to be inspired but the results were far greater than I imagined.

Growing up in central Appalachia, I did not wear the "Appalachian" badge by virtue of my birthplace, my kin or the way I spoke and neither did anyone I knew. Instead, we tried—like all kids do—to imitate the celebrities we saw on television and in magazines. Most of the time, however, I felt that I fell short of the mainstream American norm, though I couldn't have told you what that was, exactly. All I knew was that on the continuum from failure to famous, I believed I had much farther to climb because I lived—it seemed—in the middle of nowhere and spoke a very different kind of English than people on television.

One television show that seemed to get it right when it came to the values, traditions and speech with which I was familiar was Earl Hamner's *The Waltons*, a 1970's television series based on Hamner's life growing up in the Blue Ridge Mountains of Virginia. The show was set during the Depression and World War II, and a family of children who wore overalls and walked in bare feet did not depict *my* reality. Nevertheless, John-Boy Walton's dream of becoming a published writer and his family's unconditional love and encouragement mirrored my family's support of my goals. Like him, I often heard that success would be in my future if I worked hard enough.

Over the course of several episodes, John-Boy meets successful people as they travel through Walton's Mountain, taking inspiration from their individual stories; likewise, his family inspires those who seem to have everything and yet cannot find happiness. This book is meant to do that very thing for its readers. It is a book that I wish I could have read as a young adult. Though I was lucky to have a supportive family, there were formative years when I internalized the stereotypes about my region and language. It would have served me well to read that the President of NASCAR, a bestselling Appalachian author, a former NFL player and a doctor all credit their formative Appalachian cultures—and Napoleon Hill, who shares that heritage—for being where they are today.

When I went to college, I took a class called Appalachian Prose and Poetry that changed the direction of my goals because I was finally able to put a name to what connected me so strongly to my region and its culture. Through the power of literature—in which authors like James Still and Lee Smith created characters whose voices sounded like mine and who lived in places I knew—I learned that mine is a place born of struggle and heartache, settled by proud people who have learned not just how to survive but how to *thrive*.

Many of us in central and southern Appalachia were (and still are) rural people, as was Napoleon Hill and his family. I and several of my family members have lived in trailers and hollows, worked in coal and lumber or for the electric company or highway department and were baptized in the muddy waters of the Powell River. We grew tobacco and made molasses for extra money. We plant big gardens and share what we harvest. We are honest, hard-working, intelligent people.

Society has made some progress in appreciating people of all ethnicities, regions and walks of life, particularly here in Hill Country. Many colleges and universities now have Appalachian Studies programs, Appalachian literature is taught in many public schools (which was not the case twenty years ago) and scores of conferences and festivals held throughout the region serve to celebrate the various cultures that represent what we know as "Appalachia."

But old habits are hard to break. The stereotype of Appalachia as a pitiful, poor, backwoods place has incredible staying power in the minds of many who know little about the successes this region has produced. The best way to combat this image is to replace it with the reality inherent in the narratives collected here.

I took to heart the advice I heard from the men and women in these pages. Before I began writing the book, I was not as active in determining my own path as I should have been, allowing life's circumstances to chart the course for me instead of making hard choices and sticking to them. I had no one to blame for that since my upbringing was based on the principles in this book. Married as teenagers and with very little money, my parents eventually built their dream home and a solid marriage that is going strong after forty years. They raised two children whose education included the lessons learned from watching them stay dedicated to their own goals.

My mother completed her college education, though it took over twenty years because she was raising two children and working full-time. She left her job as a secretary and realized her dream of becoming a teacher. (She has since gone on to complete her doctoral degree.) My father retired from his career as an electrician several years ago and bought a saw mill; he is now building his own successful business at a time when most people would be content to sit on the front porch. Additionally, he is a member of a singing group called The Good Shepherd Quartet, who realized their dream of appearing on the Grand Ole Opry stage not once . . . but *twice*. My younger brother has followed their examples and is working his way up in a company where he has been rewarded for going the extra mile in both sales and management.

After I began these interviews, I set small goals in my personal and professional life and remained dedicated to achieving them, one by one. They were simple goals, such as completing my doctoral degree, earning tenure and buying a home in an historic neighborhood I had admired since childhood. Additionally, I worked on achieving balance among the professional, spiritual and other personal segments of my life.

While my goals may not be awe-inspiring and did not result in wealth they have contributed to my sense of peace and satisfaction, which Hill says are key tenets in achieving success. That sense of peace is the reason, I believe, that I met a kindred spirit in my husband and was blessed with a son and daughter. My family is my ultimate success, a gift that arrived once I believed in myself enough to receive it.

The day that Don and I began talking about this book, my hope was—and still is—that *Success in Hill Country* finds its way into the hands of those who have dreams as the people in this book once did and who may need the inspiration these stories can provide. As Napoleon Hill said, "Whatever the mind can conceive and believe, the mind can achieve, regardless of how many times you may have failed in the past, or how lofty your aims and hopes may be."

Welcome to Hill Country

People are wrong about you, Napoleon. You're not the worst boy in the county, only the most active. You just need to direct your energy toward accomplishing something worthwhile.

—MARTHA RAMEY BANNER, NAPOLEON HILL'S STEPMOTHER

The place that gave the world Napoleon Hill is its own success story, in many ways. Washington Irving, the author well-known for his stories "The Legend of Sleepy Hollow" and "Rip Van Winkle" even suggested in a letter dated 1839 that the country might be renamed The United States of Appalachia (or Alleghania) because the mountain chain is such a prominent feature as to represent the entire coun-try.* Though Irving's suggestion never amounted to an actual change, Appalachia's ancient mountains, familiar to the western Europeans who joined Native American settle-ments there in the eighteenth century, have sustained three

---

* Jeff Biggers, The United States of Appalachia: How Southern Mountaineers Brought Independence, Culture and Enlightenment to America, Counterpoint, 2007

hundred years' worth of pioneers, revolutionaries, artists, and activists.

In the past few decades, awareness and interest in Appalachia's people and culture has steadily grown. Appalachian authors and musicians have become so popular, for example, they now appeal to the mainstream public. Just ask bestselling author Adriana Trigiani about how Big Stone Gap, Virginia shaped her breakout novel, which will be adapted to film. Ask Grammy award-winning musician Ralph Stanley about playing Carnegie Hall. As bestselling Appalachian author (and Grundy, Virginia native) Lee Smith says, mainstream America's curiosity about the region draws attention to the talents of its people. As bits of our culture emerge across the nation, particularly in the arts, Smith contends that America is becoming "Appalachianized."

So we know what it means to be Appalachianized, but what does it *mean* to be successful? Ask any group of people their individual definitions of success and there will likely be a common denominator in their answers: everyone, it seems, is driven by the possibility of wealth. Television programming suggests that money and fame are primary forces behind ratings and thrive on the viewers' secret desires as they watch others trying to grab the golden ring.

But you'll learn more about wealth from folks like east Tennessean Charles Smiddy, who began his business at age twelve with a popcorn machine and later became a millionaire.

While Napoleon Hill's books often reference financial wealth as one of the outcomes of success, his definition of success doesn't depend entirely on money. In fact, in his book *Succeed and Grow Rich Through Persuasion*, Hill writes: "The man is rich indeed who has more friends than enemies, fears no one, and is so busy building that he has no time to devote to tearing down another's hope and plans." In *Keys to Success*, Hill doesn't talk about wealth as the *equivalent* of success, but wealth as a *by-product* of success. His definition of success can be found in the principles he developed as a blueprint for building it. Success, Hill believed, results in the lessons people learn as they work toward their goals.

In *Keys to Success*, Hill doesn't talk about wealth as the *equivalent* of success, but wealth as a *by-product* of success ... Success, Hill believed, results in the lessons people learn as they work toward their goals.

One of the ironies at work in Hill's life is that he was born in a region perceived more as poverty-ridden and ignorant than successful. In 1883, the Appalachian region was still recovering from the devastation of the Civil War and its effects on the railroads. The Deep South, where the market for Appalachian products such as livestock and food was greatest, was also ravaged. Appalachia's postwar society, according to John Williams in his book *Appalachia: a History*, was "fragmented, divided, impoverished, and violent . . . whereby undiminished population growth ran up against diminished resources."* Appalachia was also in a state of transition in the late 1800's, moving from a chiefly agrarian economy to one that would be industrialized by coal companies. But that transition would be slow, as the consequences of war continued to echo through its mountains.

---

* 2002, UNC Press, p. 181

Since its settlement, Appalachia has been cast as a region plagued by problems of its own creation, instead of a region beleaguered by outside forces. Unfortunately, those circumstances are rarely blamed for Appalachia's problems; instead, the combined stereotypes of ignorance, illiteracy, poor work ethic and unforgiving terrain have served as a more dramatic pallet for early local color writers and filmmakers who had the power to paint the region's portrait for the rest of America.

Fortunately, that didn't stop Napoleon Hill, or the generations of successful Appalachians who followed, like Dr. Miriam Fuller, the first African-American woman to be admitted to a Virginia college when segregation was still the unspoken law throughout Virginia. And Joseph Smiddy, the college's first chancellor, who admitted her.

NAPOLEON HILL: A SUCCESS STORY

For a young Napoleon Hill, coming of age at the beginning of the 20th century symbolized a series of new opportunities, among them a chance to work with Rufus Ayers, a man he held in high regard. Eighteen year-old Hill wanted to work for Ayers so badly that he offered to pay the prominent attorney for the opportunity.*

"I have just completed a business college course and am well-qualified to serve as your secretary," Hill wrote to Ayers. "Because I have no previous experience, I know that at the beginning working for you will be of more value to me than

---

* Michael J. Ritt & Kirk Landers, *A Lifetime of Riches: The Biography of Napoleon Hill,* High Roads Media, 1995, p. 19

it will be to you. Because of this I am willing to pay for the privilege of working with you." What is it about Ayers that inspired Hill to extend such a bold proposition? Perhaps it was that Ayers had served as Virginia's Attorney General, or that he was one of the state's more prominent attorneys, or that Ayers was one of the most powerful businessmen in the region. Perhaps it was because Hill's community held Ayers in such high regard.

Hill probably did not know at the time of his request how closely Ayers' upbringing resembled his own, and how closely Hill's future success would parallel that of his mentor. Whether Hill was aware of the similarities in their lives, it is certain that Ayers influenced his philosophy of success. When Hill began to research successful men for the purposes of writing his book *Think and Grow Rich*, Ayers was one of the models of success he drew upon, and for good reason.

By his late twenties, Ayers was well on his way to becoming one of the most prominent politicians and businessmen in Virginia. In 1876, the same year he purchased *The Post*, he established a charter for a railroad to be built from Bristol to Cumberland Gap. This would be the first of many acts that would lead him to be heralded as an industrial leader.

In 1879, John Imboden wrote about the untapped minerals in the coal veins of the central Appalachians. Imboden met with Pittsburgh coal investors, and persuaded them that southwest Virginia could be the "Pittsburgh of the south." However, according to Richard B. Drake's *A History of Appalachia*, the area was so mountainous it was known as the "Switzerland of America." Without a way in and out, the coal would remain buried deep inside unyielding, steep, and rocky terrain. Since Ayers was building a railroad, he was a key contact person for coal investors looking to mine the mountains, and fought other communities' efforts to acquire the rail lines in order to keep them in southwest Virginia.

Ayers saw wonderful opportunities for industry in Big Stone Gap and organized the Virginia Coal and Iron Company in 1881, with Ayers serving as both director and vice president at age 32. Among the many companies he would build in the next two decades, Ayers organized and directed the Virginia, Tennessee and Carolina Steel and Iron Company. The company topped $2,500,000 and took over coal lands in Wise, Dickenson, and Buchanan counties as well as mineral lands in Tennessee and North Carolina.

Ayers moved his family to Big Stone Gap, where he built a $25,000 home—a mansion by 1890 standards—constructed of sandstone and limestone. Hand-carved red oak trimmed the interior.* During the next decade and a half, he would organize and run twelve businesses, maintain law offices in Bristol and Big Stone Gap, and return to his role as editor after buying the *Big Stone Post* newspaper at a public auction (later renamed *The Post*.) He generously divided portions of his income among charities, and donated to college funds. In 1901, Ayers met an enthusiastic young man whose life and accomplishments would resemble his own in many ways.

Napoleon Hill's persuasive request for a job impressed Ayers, prompting him to hire Hill with pay. Hill assumed the role of a

---

* Ayers' stately home in Big Stone Gap is now the Southwest Virginia Museum Historical State Park, which Stands—along with the foundations of what southwest Virginia became—as a symbol of a man who conceieved of many dreams for the region, believed he could accomplish them, and achieved them, one by one.

bright young executive in both appearance and action, and was quickly promoted to chief clerk at a Richlands coal mine.

In his unpublished memoirs, Hill narrated an event that had a profound impact on him, as well as Ayers. It began when the brother of the coal mine manager dropped a loaded revolver in the lobby of a hotel, accidentally killing the bellboy. Hill immediately went to the scene and made arrangements for the burial. The man responsible for the boy's death worked as a cashier at one of Ayers' banks. He fled, leaving the bank vaults open. Ayers instructed Hill to assume responsibility for the bank and the money and to compensate any shortage from Ayers' personal account.

Hill was impressed with Ayers' trust, while Ayers was impressed with Hill's honesty and managerial skills. He was immediately given the mine manager's job. To be sure, Hill's brief career with Ayers' company made an impression that would last a lifetime.

LEARNING FROM THE LIVES OF OTHERS

Andrew Carnegie, who was one of the models of success Hill interviewed as he developed his own principles, implored Hill to continue his research on how to achieve success. He directed Hill to compare his success with "the experience of other men who have been recognized as successes in many fields of endeavor, in order that you may give the world a successful philosophy of sufficient flexibility that it will serve the needs of all people, regardless of their calling or purpose in life."

Some readers may question how the people profiled in this book were chosen, when there are so many notable Appalachians who have been successful in one way or another and who have also seen mainstream success. While it is impossible to name every one, I have followed Carnegie's advice to Hill by interviewing successful Appalachians from in and around Hill's birthplace and from several different fields, examining how they define success and how they have realized their definitions of success in their lives using Hill's principles. End of chapter notes include notable Appalachians who have achieved national and international recognition for their groundbreaking successes.

The successful people in this book come from a hardworking, proud and independent region. The voices in these narratives will tell you about their recipes for success. You'll hear from Mike Helton, President of NASCAR, who says that success is like a "family recipe that you're proud of." Carefully combining the right ingredients at just the right time will result in a good product that will make everyone come back for more. "The secret," Helton cautions, "is to not give out too many secrets so when they do come back to get them, they come back to *you*."*

This book will provide a few of those secrets from those who have first-hand knowledge of why and how they work.

Why should you listen to folks from Hill Country?

The men and women in these pages come from a diverse, working-class region that is deeply rooted in their ancestors' tradition of digging out a living in rocky terrain. They come from a region that has never been associated with success or wealth, because many "foreigners" (the name given to those

---

* Public address at the University of Virginia's College at Wise, 2004

born outside of its boundaries) fail to look beyond the stereo-types. They come from a place that contains mysterious, shad-owed pockets between the hollows and hills, a place that holds true to culture and tradition, a place with multiple, misun-derstood dialects that serve to keep some Appalachians teth-ered to their homes and families no matter how far they travel. They have let their cultures inform their identities and inspire their creativity. The people in this book have achieved a range of successes, from modest to celebrity. They are from Hill Country, and they've become successful both because of—and in spite of—what it means to be Appalachian in America.

The people in this book have achieved a range of successes, from modest to celebrity. They are from Hill Country, and they've become successful both because of—and in spite of— what it means to be Appalachian in America.

MYTH AND TRUTH IN THE BACKCOUNTRY

Great achievement is born of a struggle. —NAPOLEON HILL

If ever a region or community of people embodied Napoleon Hill's principles, his home place in central Appalachia cer-tainly does. Since its settlement the topography of Appalachia has presented formidable challenges that only strengthened the resolve of its people. The labor force is continually at the mercy of an unstable economy, which means that—like any area of the United States—there are pockets of Appalachia where those most affected by its challenges continue to live generation after generation.

When the coal industry began to decline in the 1950's, Appalachians migrated north and west to look for work. The region was notorious for being "the place to leave" and Route 23 to Ohio became known as "Hillbilly Highway."* Appalachia lost a staggering portion of its population to industrial centers in Michigan and Ohio. Since then, it has continued to struggle with supporting its labor force as coal production continues to decline or become more mechanized. Of the roughly 400 counties that comprise the region according to the federal government, central Appalachia has the highest concentrated poverty rate of the entire region, namely in eastern Kentucky and southern West Virginia† (where, ironically, the largest amount of coal is mined.)

Nevertheless, Hill Country is still a region where its principles—and its people—continue to flourish. While success stories will be the *primary* focus of this book, it's important to examine how these particular stereotypes emerged, why they persist, and why those in this book succeeded in spite of them.

When Napoleon Hill was born in the late 19th century, his birthplace of central Appalachia was, as described in Hill's biography, "almost completely isolated from the frenetic changes taking place in America's cities and towns. To reach it from the outside world, one had to navigate . . . through thick forests, deep valleys and gorges and remote hollows."‡ Though

---

* Williams, 2002

† Appalachian Regional Commission, 2011

‡ Ritt, Jr. & Landers, 1995

Appalachia changed dramatically over time, this description has, unfortunately, remained the standard for both the land and its people, overshadowing its success stories. As Appalachian author Sharyn McCrumb describes it, the west is romanticized in film and television, while the central and southern Appalachians are depicted in children with dirty faces living in mountain shacks. "Cities are judged by their richest inhabitants," McCrumb says, "and rural areas by their poorest . . ."* One of the truths this book reveals is that anyone can rise above stereotypes.

How did the Appalachians in these pages become so successful? Because they embody many of the principles for success outlined by Napoleon Hill in his book *Keys to Success*:

+ Definiteness of Purpose
+ Mastermind Alliance
+ Attractive Personality
+ Applied Faith
+ Going The Extra Mile
+ Personal Initiative
+ Positive Mental Attitude
+ Controlled Enthusiasm
+ Teamwork
+ Lessons from Adversity and Defeat
+ Creative Vision
+ Sound Health
+ Budgets for both Time and Money
+ Cosmic Habitforce

---

* Public Address, 2003

These fourteen principles can be found in the following profiles of Appalachian achievers. Some will even reference Hill. It's no coincidence that Napoleon Hill, a Wise County, Virginia native, is the architect and author of a plan for success that is used all over the globe. His principles apply to everyone, but as these profiles will show, there's something special about the success stories of those who appear to have the odds against them.

Whether you're from Kentucky or California, Tokyo or London, whether you're African-American or Caucasian, lower class or upper class, read these stories from people who credit both Napoleon Hill *and* their cultural birthplace for their achievements. Then, go and write your own success story.

CHAPTER 1

Success in Sports

Win without boasting, lose without [whining], and others will soon respect you. Athletics can make this a habit in many people, but even if you have never set foot on a playing field or a court, you can inspire others . . . —NAPOLEON HILL

Springtime in Hill Country ushers in blossoms and lush green hills, while black and white checkered flags and famed numbers sprout among lawns, billboards, car windows. In fact, NASCAR legends like Rusty Wallace began their careers in the heart of Hill Country at the Lonesome Pine Raceway in Coeburn, Virginia. Just an hour's drive from Napoleon Hill's birthplace, the Bristol Motor Speedway will host thousands of fans who flock to central Appalachia, many of whom follow their favorite drivers along the racing circuit. A sport second only to the NFL in television ratings, NASCAR is a billion-dollar industry headed by Mike Helton, who also grew up in Hill Country.

MICHAEL HELTON,
President of Nascar

NASCAR President Michael Helton says that growing up in Washington County, Virginia was an asset because Appalachia's values have so much to do with Hill's principles. "Before I even knew it," he says, "I was learning about fairness and honesty . . . patience and tolerance . . . [the] basics of life."

The NASCAR legacy began as a hobby on the dirt tracks and beaches of the southeast, led by what Helton calls "backwoods antics." William H.G. France, who participated in those races, saw their potential for commercial success. Helton compares "Big Bill" France to Henry Ford, whose business was modeled on creating a product that was both available and affordable. "He didn't invent stock car racing," Helton said of France, "but he saw a need for an organization that could deliver, promote, and assure that racetracks that wanted a show were able to collect enough owners and vehicles and go to the tracks. In 1948, he sat down with friends in a hotel in Daytona Beach and 'banged out' NASCAR. He began an organization with a simple effort: to create a good product—competition on the racetrack—that America wanted to watch."*

Helton began his career in NASCAR as a part-timer at the Bristol Motor Speedway. Using Hill's principles, he worked his way up over the years at several tracks before becoming Vice-President of Competition at NASCAR in 1994 at the age of 40. In 1997, he was appointed Senior Vice-President,

---

* Public Address, The University of Virginia's College at Wise, 2003

Chief Operating Officer, and in 2000, he became president of a corporation that, according to Helton, has 75 million fans and the second largest television audience (behind the NFL) today. Helton credits Hill Country for the values that led to his success.

In Mike Helton's words . . .

How would you define success?
Being happy with yourself. Being happy with the world around you and what you've accomplished and what you're comfortable with. I think everybody's levels of successes are different than mine and so I think it really just comes down to being happy with what you've achieved.

What was the burning desire that led you to where you are now?
My burning desire was the passion for the sport that I'm involved in. It wasn't necessarily ever a goal or a mission to reach this level in my career as much as it was to be a part of this sport and work in it and make a career in it. So I think my burning passion was more about the intrigue and the passion that I had for being involved in NASCAR.

Who are the people who have helped you become successful?
I think a lot of it starts back before I even knew it with my parents and my brothers. Certainly, I can often reflect back to some teachers whose importance I didn't realize at the time

but now I realize their influence. Then, it became different people inside the industry that I felt had great experience and knowledge, and whether I liked them or not, I still had respect for their knowledge and experience and I would be influenced by that.

The single individual that I can point to that had the most influence in my career and where I am today is Bill France, the son of the founder of NASCAR. He was my mentor for so many years and the one who taught me so many characteristics that I think I have been able to be more successful in my everyday life.

What do you think is the most significant personality characteristic in becoming successful?
I would say that hidden qualities have the most significance in achieving success, such as flexibility, sincerity, and promptness, courtesy, and tact. Those are traits that people don't immediately recognize as being appreciated. I think sometimes you get in your own way of being successful if you're so hard-driven by your own opinion. Then, you do not take the opportunity to see others' opinions.

Tolerance, humor and emotional control are very important. Humility is a wonderful one. I think it's a benefit for the greatest leaders in the world to be humble.

Hill talks about going the extra mile, doing more than is expected of you. Do you feel that characterizes how you work?
I don't have a perimeter of what's expected. I've never worked with a sense of an eight-hour day or a checklist of twenty

things that had to get done correctly. I've always looked at what I do as an open-ended project. I get a chance to lie down at night and recharge my batteries, and go right back at it the next day. It's hard for me to answer a question about going the extra mile when I don't think there's any such thing. I think you should put everything you've got into everything you do. My approach is I do it because I feel like that's the right thing to do and it doesn't matter how long it takes.

So how do you maintain a positive mental attitude, particularly with the more challenging aspects of your job?
Early on in my career I would have challenges with having to deal with tough situations, particularly when it came to being the judge and jury of an individual situation or a group of situations. Over time, I've accepted the fact that in the NASCAR industry, there has to be someone who is the authority and takes the responsibility for making tough decisions. That, in our case, happens to be us as an organization, and I happen to be the president of it, and I happen to be the guy who leads those decision-making processes.

I have come to accept—as much as *learn*—that somebody has to do it and a lot of individuals, whether they're fans or participants in the sport, depend on someone to make those decisions. It's not so much about keeping a positive mindset as it is staying focused and creating a result—hopefully the *correct* result.

How do you stay focused?
My way of staying focused is to remember that this issue needs to be resolved with a consciousness of the constituen-

cies that the resolution will affect. It could be a single incident involving an individual or a team, but the reaction to
and the resolution of that issue are going to have ripple effects
for a long period of time in the entire industry. So, I stay
focused by reminding myself that the resolution is expected
and will also become the example that the next incident will
be referred to.

**Part of being successful is learning how to fail, accept
defeat, and keep going. Have you learned from defeat or
adversity?**

Yes, I have, and I'm sure I'll continue to learn throughout my
career. I hope I'll learn less than I have in the past, but every
time you lose or are facing adversity you ask yourself, 'Why?'
And in asking yourself 'why' you learn your mistake. You learn
why you did not accomplish what you wanted or why you're in
the position you're in. While you learn that, you're now better prepared to accomplish other goals because you know that
action created a negative result for you. You learn from that.
The experience teaches you.

The lessons that stick with you the best are the ones that
you suffer from and that means you've lost or there's an adver-
sarial result. It's like grabbing a boiling pot of water, which
you remember more than drinking a glass of cool water when
you're thirsty.

Every time you lose or are facing adversity you ask yourself,
'Why?' And in asking yourself 'why' you learn your mistake.

Do you have a habit for maintaining your physical and mental health? Do you think that's important?

Yes, I do think it's important because if you're not feeling good or you're not healthy then you're distracted from your surroundings. I pay more attention today than ever to my exercise and diet. For mental health, in addition to depending on faith (whatever your definition may be) you need to be satisfied with your current level of knowledge or always eager to add to it. I entertain myself by learning things that are interesting to me. It could be what I was supposed to have learned back when I was in school and didn't pay attention, such as a new part of the country or a new international destination. It may just be a good book that tells part of the history of our country or maybe it's just a pure fiction that is interesting enough to stimulate the mind.

Do you feel like growing up in central Appalachia was a hindrance to your success, a motivating factor, or both?

I don't think it was a hindrance. In my career and what I do, it was an asset because of the values that exist in Appalachia. It's the heart and soul of faith. Having had the opportunity to travel all across this country and seeing other regions and attitudes that are different than the Appalachian area, I've had the opportunity to compare what I was raised in to what I see today in other areas. While I see other areas of the world change, every time I get to come back home I see our values are still strong. Now, I'm not a rocket scientist and I'm not a professor in some high-tech laboratory creating software or the next incredible medicine for a disease, but in doing what

I do—which is to balance the rule-making process and the activity of the sport—I think that being from the Appalachian area is a great asset to me because before I even knew it, I was learning about values, fairness, honesty . . . the basics of life.

In the Appalachian region, you spend more time exposed to the basics of life than you might in other regions of the country where life moves a lot faster. I'm not saying that to put Appalachia down; I'm saying that to brag about it. Patience, tolerance, and a good foundation are at the core of an individual's success and that's what I think individuals who come from Appalachia have. They have a strong, basic foundation and I know they get it there.

What advice would you give someone who is looking to you as a model for success, especially someone from Appalachia?
If I had to look back and list my accomplishments, I think what I would have to list is almost the same answer to your last question and that's learning patience and tolerance. That's easier said than done. I understand a teenager or even an individual in their early twenties being anxious to get out and do things beyond the perimeters of their region because in today's world—with technology and television making the world so small—you're exposed to others' ways of life more quickly than when I was being brought up in the Appalachian area, so it's a greater challenge.

My advice would be to think about the effect of your decisions and how they're going to affect the people in your life. It starts with you, but also spreads out to all the other constituencies in your life. Now, if you're a 12, 13, or 16 year-old it's hard to identify those people, but certainly it starts with your parents and siblings. So, the next step you take or the major decision you make shouldn't be just about the impact on you, but it should be about the impact that the decision will have on your community and your world. That's where it starts.

You have to believe in yourself. What helps you believe in yourself is having the external support group of family members and friends, as well as confidence and faith. My advice for anyone who wants to be successful in life is to understand that the definitions of success are very broad and diverse. Don't let your own definition of success be driven by someone else's. Commit yourself to being open-minded, to learning, to being committed and being respectful and all these characteristics that the Appalachian area instills in you. Let those work for you. Don't work against them, and don't fight them. Then, whatever decision you make that may keep you in the Appalachian area or take you to the corners of the world, you'll be better prepared for it.

CARROLL DALE,
NFL Receiver, Los Angeles Rams, Green Bay Packers, Minnesota Vikings

Friday nights in fall means crisp air punctuated with puffs of breath, stadium lights that blaze through the night for miles, and the echoes of a thousand cheering voices following a football down the field. For many of these young players, football is their ticket to college. For some, the dream is to 'go pro,' but less than one percent of Division I players nationwide will end up in the NFL. Yet, Hill Country produced Thomas and Julius Jones from Big Stone Gap, Virginia as well as Heath Miller, from Sword's Creek, Virginia.

Carroll Dale, a native of Wise County, works in an office that is literally covered with symbols of recognition; stepping into the room is like walking into a Hall of Fame (you'll find his name in two of them), but Dale dismisses it all with a wave of his hand. These are *things*, he reminds me, that ultimately mean very little in terms of worth. What matters, as his story reveals, is the way one goes about achieving them.

But these *things* do symbolize Dale's admirable successes. He began his football career at Virginia Polytechnic and State University as an offensive and defensive end, and went on to become Tech's first All-American, among the many other accolades he received. He then spent five years with the Los Angeles Rams before he was traded to the Green Bay Packers in 1965. He began a winning career under legendary coach Vince Lombardi, who led the Packers to victory in Super Bowls I and II. As number 84, Dale set the all-time record for average yards per reception. He was inducted into the Packer Hall of Fame in 1979. Dale finished his NFL career with the Minnesota Vikings before returning to his roots in Wise County, where those plaques, trophies, and photographs suggest that there's an inspiring success story to be told.

It's a success story that embodies several important ingredients from Napoleon Hill's recipe, particularly applied faith, teamwork, and learning from adversity.

In Carroll Dale's words . . .

How do you define success?
I define success as giving it your best effort, including sound preparation. In other words, it's not necessarily whether or not you win, but it boils down to giving it your best effort and if you fall short of your goal then I still define that as success.

What do you count among your greatest accomplishments?
I committed my life to Christ at an early age (eighth grade) and that enabled me to set proper goals which thwarted a lot of detours.

What obstacles did you encounter along the way?
Coming from a rural area and a small high school with meager resources at home probably created low self-esteem. I remember thinking I probably couldn't go to college like kids in Richmond and other places. My mom was a stay-athome mom and my dad was a coal miner early on, and then he ended up being the custodian here [in Wise] at JJ Kelly High School. We were too poor to pay attention!

How did you combat these obstacles?
When opportunities came by I accepted them with the attitude of giving it my best effort. If I didn't make it, at least I tried.

You're well known for your achievements in football. What
was the burning desire that led you to follow this path?
I watched upperclassmen going to football practice when I
was in elementary school. We did not have sandlot football, so
eighth grade was the first opportunity. I decided I wanted to
play. I set that goal. Then, I was made to realize through my
mom's help that if I didn't pass my schoolwork, I wouldn't be
able to play, so that motivated me. And as I said, I accepted
Christ at a young age. For some reason, I just wanted to play.
There was no football background in my family, and certainly
we didn't have TV coverage.

What was your plan in getting there?
Through spiritual experience, that enabled me to do the
proper goal setting, as far as priorities in the proper order, and
of course the willingness to work hard.

Whom did you consult?
Parents play a big part, as well as teachers, coaches, pastors,
your church family—it's hard to go back and pick out one
individual. It's a combination of people who were helpful along
the way. If you take the right attitude you're drawn to other
positive thinking people.

Applied Faith and Decision-Making
High school was probably the toughest time in my spiritual
life. I was nicknamed "preacher." That wouldn't bother me
now, but *then* it probably caused me some heartache. Even
so, Christian principles were great to live by because it kept

me out of other things and helped me to at least make decent grades and sound decisions. By junior year, I knew I couldn't go to college unless I got a football scholarship, and I decided that if I got the opportunity I would try.

I made decent grades and had several opportunities to attend college at UVA., Georgia, Clemson, Tennessee and Virginia Tech. When I decided to go to Tech, the coach told me they would give me an opportunity for an education and play all the football I wanted to play.

I wanted to go into engineering, and I figured that math and English are the tough courses (and probably still are.) So, I went to summer school. The day I arrived, some of the football players—upperclassmen—were going from Roanoke to Blacksburg to play in a softball tournament. I said I would go watch, so I drove up there with them. They played the softball game, and of course they broke out the beer. It kind of caught me by surprise. I just told them no, thank you. But I probably would not have gone had I known that was going to happen.

When Opportunity Knocks . . .

The fall practice started the preseason. Even though freshmen were eligible the coach didn't believe in playing freshmen. One guy who played my position flunked summer school and was not eligible. Then, an All-Conference receiver had a career-ending ankle injury, so there were two veteran receivers out. At that point, they didn't have a lot of depth so they had to bring me in before the opening game of the season.

We were playing Eastern Carolina. The player in front of me sprained his ankle. I played the rest of that game. Then we played Tulane the next week, and I started. At that time, the rule was if you left the game during the quarter you could not re-enter the game until the next quarter. So we had to play 60 minutes. We had to play special teams, defense, offense, everything. I started that game and played every minute of the next 38 games after that. There I was, right out of high school, starting in New Orleans against Tulane in the Sugar Bowl stadium.

Going Pro ...

In my junior and senior years, I started to get questionnaires from professional teams including Canada. That's the year the AFL (American Football League) started. The Los Angeles Rams drafted me. The player in front of me got hurt and I started the second game of the regular season. Here's opportunity again. I caught five passes, one of them a touchdown pass.

Being human, I was up a little early Sunday morning, waiting to read about the Rams' new-found receiver in the paper. Monday, we had a light workout, and I pulled a hamstring muscle. That helped bring me back down to earth.

Green Bay Packer Football and Coach Vince Lombardi

The receiver coach I had in LA had been, for a week or so, employed by the Green Bay Packers. He left LA in '63 and went to Green Bay as a receiver coach. He helped make the decision to trade the all-pro receiver and keep me. That was a dream come true for two reasons. They were contenders: they had won the championship in '61 and '62, and they had been second in their conference in '63 and '64. They were my pick.

The second reason gets back to the rural. Green Bay was 50,000 [in population] at that time, and you could get across town in 10–15 minutes. So it was the smallest city—still is—in the NFL. I was back in my rural surroundings and much more comfortable than in the other places.

Humility is one of the top traits for staying grounded. Remember the guy who said, 'I'm so humble, I'm proud of it!' It doesn't work that way. A lot of it—especially in professional sports—is about the team and depends on who you're with.

When Vince Lombardi came to Green Bay, he was experienced enough that he really understood players. He had expertise in judging players. He was consistent. He would say, 'You're my quarterback this week,' and if he was going to change, he wouldn't yank you out during the game. He'd come and say, 'You're having trouble; it's time I give someone else a chance.' Everything he did was for the good of the team. He never let emotion or how he felt about you personally get involved. You could be trying to talk contract with him and end up in a disagreement. But when it came time for the game, if you were the best player at that position, you'd be playing and nothing would boil over. He wouldn't be ticked off at you for not agreeing with him about the contract.

He was a devoutly religious man who went to Mass regularly. In fact, my maneuver to get an extra few dollars from him was to say, 'Coach, I tithe and if you'll send a check to my church in Bristol, I'll agree to sign this contract because I'm going to give ten percent of it to them, anyway.' That accomplished two things: my contract did not include that money, and he kept me to the minimal raise that he wanted to keep people under control. The Vikings kept that clause in the contract.

Inspiration and Motivation, Lombardi-Style:
"Religion, Family, and Green Bay Packer Football"

When we went to the Super Bowl, Coach Lombardi's speech to our team was, 'This is the only opportunity this team has as it exists to be a world champion. If you don't take advantage of it, you'll be remembered as a loser.'

Coach Lombardi taught priorities, also. Every year he would say, 'Gentlemen, there should be only three things on your mind. Number one: your church, God, or religion; number two, your family; and number three, Green Bay Packer football, in that order and nothing else.' We had the only Super Bowl ring (II), which I'm wearing, that has scripture.

He always said, 'It takes a greater team to repeat as a champion than to become a champion.' We were going for our third world championship. This ring challenges you to stay on top because when you're on top everyone is trying to knock you off. "Run to win" means this is the only Super Bowl Ring guaranteed to have scripture on it. We were in a meeting in 1967 and he said, 'Gentlemen, Saint Paul said in a race there are many runners, but only one will win the prize, so run to win.' I was the chapel leader, so he asked, 'Have you heard of that, Carroll?' In meetings there was only one answer that you could give and that was, 'Yes, sir!' because the only other answer meant making excuses. I went straight home and looked it up. It's Corinthians I, 9:24.

Positive mental attitude, faith, and sense of justice are at the top of the list of the most important personality traits. Then tact, tone of voice, habit of smiling, and sense of humor are important. Appropriate use of words is very important. Some people have more ability with words and effective speech. Emotional control ranks very high, too. As a side note, I include *effective* showmanship because I detest it (unless you're in entertainment), especially when it comes to sports. It's very individual, not thinking of the rest of the team.

Vince Lombardi knew how to motivate and part of it was intimidation. He had a big voice, and he could do it in such a way that he got your attention. He had this great ability to know which players to kick in the seat of the pants and which to put his arm around, so to speak, or pat on the back. He knew that he could "chew butt" when we won, and that's when he did it. That's when he really made corrections. See, when you win, nobody's blaming you for losing. If we lost, he still made corrections, but he didn't humiliate anybody. He knew enough about the psychology of players that he knew he had to keep us from getting 'blown up' and thinking we were good. You better be concentrating Tuesday, Wednesday, Thursday; he wanted you ready for the game. If he knew you weren't concentrating during the week, you weren't respecting your opponent. I've watched and played on all levels, and when you don't get ready to play the game and respect your opponent, then look out: you're going to get nailed.

Applied Faith

Goal setting with the proper priorities comes with putting the spiritual first.

When I was a rookie with the Rams, they had a course called "Executive Dynamics" and they used *Psycho-Cybernetics* by Maxwell Maltz as the textbook. He was a plastic surgeon and the gist of his message was that he could make people beautiful on the outside, but that did not necessarily make them beautiful on the inside. The course included affirmation and visualization, which I think is important. When you write down goals and put them on paper, you're visualizing yourself being there. When it comes to sports, it's even more important, because you visualize success. Anytime negative thoughts come into your mind, it's mind control. You have to put those out of your mind and replace them with successful thoughts.

I haven't forgotten this all these years. When you go to bed at night, the affirmations go something like this: 'I have warm regards for all people at all times' (which is the spiritual); and 'Love your neighbors, love your enemies' (which is not all that easy). Then you visualize your successes. As the visualization happens, you drift off to sleep. If you are having sleep problems, it will cleanse your mind. I used this with my kids, too. A lot of the problems we have to deal with are mind control and thinking positively.

Many of us try to think of the big mountain instead of climbing the little hill at the base of the mountain. You have to look at it in steps and not be overwhelmed.

You can sit and visualize all you want to, and all of us can dream and think 'What would I do if . . . ' You can't just stop there; it takes action.

You can sit and visualize all you want to, and all of us can dream and think 'What would I do if . . . ' You can't just stop there; it takes action.

Going the Extra Mile . . .

I've always been willing to do anything that I would ask others to do. For example, at Virginia Tech, about six years ago I was doing the Golf Tournament Spring Swing at the country club. We stopped and went into the restroom. The commode was running. I took the top off to jiggle it and saw credit cards. I stuck my hand down in the tank to take out the credit cards and a driver's license and it was Frank Beamer's [Virginia Tech's head football coach]. Frank was ahead of me a hole or two and that was after they beat Auburn at the Sugar Bowl— they had a Sugar Bowl ring. I found out that he had put his watch, his ring, and about $350 in a bag in the golf cart. When he stopped and went inside, somebody took the cash, the ring, and the watch and dumped the credit cards in the tank. When somebody flushed it before me, the credit cards caught under the flap.

What motivates you to action once you have an idea?

Thinking about it probably to the point of obsession. If I hadn't made a spiritual commitment early, I probably wouldn't be alive today. If I had been out partying, I would have been the best drunk on the planet. I would probably have been a goner.

How do you maintain a positive mental attitude in the face of challenging circumstances?

Perseverance and never giving up. If you told me I couldn't do it, I'd try to show you I could. Get knocked down, get back up, and get back in the game as quickly as you can. It's easy to give up. You need to have realistic goals.

What techniques do you use to stay focused on your goals?
I focus totally on the goals and avoid the distractions. In my desire to play football, I avoided girls until I got to be a sophomore, because I thought it would be a distraction. That's probably a true statement for guys in athletics. You see them fall in love, and they have talent, and they're goners. It happens often. It wasn't even a temptation: (1) because of the spiritual, and (2) because I was possessed with a love of sports. Whatever the season was, that's what I was involved in.

What's your method for reasoning through a decision or problem?
Prayer and meditation. I've been very fortunate sometimes when decisions were made and I'm not sure how it happened.

How do you work with others to achieve your goals?
Becoming aware that it takes others to get the job done, especially when it comes to team sports. You are dependent on the other people. It's always good to try and let those people know that you appreciate what they do. That comes with courtesy and humility. It goes with being a positive example.

Describe a time when you learned from adversity or defeat:
I was with the Los Angeles Rams in my second year and they traded an offensive receiver that had made All-Pro two years before. They kept me and I was a starter. The second game of the year, we were playing the Pittsburgh Steelers. I ran what we call a hook pattern—you go about 12 or 15 yards and turn

and come back for the ball—and the ball hit me on my numbers. 72,000 people went 'Oh!' at the same time. To make a long story short, for about eight weeks I couldn't catch a ball in a basket. It got worse.

In Chicago we were playing the Bears, and I ran down to the goal line, wide open, and I squeezed it and [he gestures to show that he dropped the ball.] I had to go back and really evaluate things. I came to the following realization. I had my priorities out of order because I was thinking about myself instead of the team or the spiritual. I was so low that I had to say, 'Lord, help me. I want to put the team first and my prayer before the game is going to be for the protection of everybody, and that I go out and play for your glory and for the good of the team. If I catch it, fine and if I don't, I gave it my best effort.' I also realized that I had gotten away from the fundamentals of catching. I don't know why the coach didn't see it, but I started trying to catch the ball in my arms instead of using my hands. Thank goodness there was one game left in the year, though we lost. We were playing the Baltimore Colts and I caught a long, 68 yard pass. It was through that I had to really learn a hard lesson.

How do you get inspired?

It's good to associate with people who have experience in a certain area that you have an idea in. Have a great respect for that experience. Like Napoleon Hill, you find successful or positive thinking people and try to learn from what they've done. If they've been there, it can save you a lot of heartache sometimes. It's also very inspiring to hear somebody's success story. And that's also very positive.

What are your habits for maintaining mental and physical health?

I avoided situations or activities that could injure me. In football, you realize that it's all physical. I still like to play golf. If your knees, ankles, and feet don't work, you don't do it. It's painful anyway, at best. Add to that all the other distractions such as drugs and alcohol. It's disappointing to see mentally and physically talented young people self-destruct. That's literally what they're doing and it's discouraging and a shame.

What is your best advice for budgeting time and money?

Easy: don't over-commit either time or money. When I first went to Green Bay and we won, I felt like I had to take every appearance opportunity, especially to witness to high school kids. Someone told me, 'Look, you've got obligations—family, kids.' The guy I talked to was gone so much that one of his children ended up having a drug problem. He was older and was able to tell me, 'Set your schedule for once a week.' It affected my health; I ended up with an eye problem, which was a swelling of the retina behind one of my eyes from the stress of trying to do everything.

How was your environment a factor in achieving success?

Coming from a rural area created an inferiority complex for me. I became aware that everybody's human, no matter where they're from and if you are going to do something, your environment doesn't have to hold you back if you have the physical and mental ability to get it done.

How has your environment influenced you as you achieved success?

I've returned to the mountains. There's not enough money in the world to send me to a metropolitan area now.

In college, I received a letter from a guy offering me a job. I told him that I appreciated it, but I wanted to play pro-football. In my junior year in the spring, we were playing an alumni football game. I was coming back to block, and the player saw me coming and he turned and threw an elbow and caught me in the face. It caved my sinuses, and I later lost teeth. My eye swelled shut. My five year-old neighbor across the street from where I lived said, 'I don't want to play football when I grow up.'

I had to drop out of school during the spring quarter and decided to go to summer school and make it up. I'd been working for the railroad in the summer and I asked if I could work until the last session of summer school. They said, 'We have a job for you in the summer, but not right now.' So, I remembered the correspondence I had with the guy previously so I called him and told him what had happened. I said, 'If you're willing, I'd be glad to come down and work with you until I have to go back to summer school.' Basically, that's how I ended up being back here.

By being in the area and making friends, I got involved in the coal business, which I did for 17 years. I said some things earlier about planning and why things happen. The hit upside the head brought me back where I really wanted to be, and with opportunity in the coal business. I had a cousin in the business, so I got involved in two jobs (one in Kentucky). I owned a couple of trucks and ran a job that did surface mining on the college property.

In 1988, Dr. Jimmy Knight [who was then chancellor of UVA-Wise] asked me to serve on a committee [appointed to study the feasibility of creating a football program at the college.] We hired a coach, but the college did not have a full-time athletic director. So, they did a search and I got the job and came on board here in 1991.

Looking back at things that happened, I didn't miss a day's work at either place. Why I ended up in Bristol, why I ended up in the coal business (which I never dreamed), and why I ended up at the college (which I never visualized) leads to the question, 'Was there a higher being involved in all of this?' Personally, I think so.

It wasn't that I sat down many years ago and said, 'I want to be a coal operator, or an athletic director or a fundraiser for a college.' But it has turned out that I have had a great deal of fun and enjoyment. Most of all, to come back where my folks live and where I was born and raised has been fine, and to be able to give something back to the area that I'm from, that is my roots. I'm amazed when people have a little success monetarily and they want to move away. I don't care how much money I have; I don't want to do that.

What advice would you give to those who want to follow your example?
Set high goals, avoid negative people, visit with positive or successful people and set the proper priorities: spiritual life, goals, work ethic and balance in your lifestyle. If you have obligations you need to honor them. You need to pray hard, work hard, and play hard.

Hill Country Athletes[*]

- **Mary Lou Retton** was born in Fairmont, West Virginia and was the first American woman to win an individual gold medal in Olympic gymnastics and the youngest inductee and first gymnast into the Olympic Hall of Fame (1985). She was also the first woman to be featured on a box of Wheaties. In 1993 she was named the Most Popular Athlete in America in an Associated Press national survey and she was inducted into the International Gymnastics Hall of Fame in 1997.

- **Willie Horton** was born in Arno, Virginia in 1942. A designated hitter and left fielder in Major League Baseball, Horton played for six American League teams, primarily the Detroit Tigers. Nicknamed "Willie the Wonder," Horton's 325 career home runs and a lifetime batting average of .273 made him a leading figure in the League. On July 15, 2000 the Detroit Tigers retired number 23, placing Horton in a choice group that includes former Tigers players Ty Cobb, Charlie Gehringer, Hank Greenberg, Al Kaline, and Hal Newhouser. The Tigers also erected a thirteen-foot statue of him in Comerica Park. Since 2003, Horton has served as a Special Assistant to Tigers President/CEO/General Manager Dave Dombrowski. Horton and former teammate Al Kaline threw out the first pitch of the 2006 World Series at Comerica Park.

[*] Information on notable people following interviews throughout this book comes from the Southwest Virginia Museum and Encyclopedia of Appalachia (Eds. Rudy Abramson and Jean Haskell, University of Tennessee Press, 2006).

- **Glenn Roberts** was born in Glamorgan, Virginia in 1912 and attended school in Pound. Roberts played varsity basketball (1931-35) at Emory & Henry College scoring 2,013 points in 104 games for a per game average of 19.4 points. His scoring set a new record and still stands for play prior to the 1937 revision of the center-jump rule, which called for walking the ball back to the center-line after every basket made and with the clock still running. His scoring total and per-game average was featured in Ripleys' "Believe it or Not" in 1936. One significant reason for Glenn Roberts' prolific scoring was his use of a jump-shot, and he was the first player to put the "jump shot" to practical use. Glenn Roberts received many professional offers from National Basketball League (NBL) and other professional teams, but chose instead to coach basketball at Norton High School in Norton, Virginia. In the two years he coached (1936 and 1937) his team won the district championship. He was chosen by the Firestone Non-Skids of the NBL to play for the 1938-39 season. Firestone won the NBL Eastern Division championship with a 30 and 2 record. They then won the NBL Championship by beating the Western Division champions (Oshkosh All-Stars) in a best of 5 series. Their .934 winning percentage for the regular season is the highest winning percentage in the history of the NBL and the NBA.

- **Ollan Cassell** was born in Nickelsville, Virginia and attended Appalachia High School. Cassell began running the quarter-mile at the University of Houston. In 1962, he won gold medals in the 400 m and 4x400 m relay and a silver medal in the 4x100 m relay at the World Military Championships. At the 1963 Pan-American Games, Cassell won two gold medals in the relays and was second in 200 m and sixth in 100 m. At the 1964 Tokyo Summer

Olympics, Cassell was a semifinalist in 400 m and ran the opening leg in the American 4x400 m relay team, which won the gold medal with a new world record of 3:00.7. Cassell won his second (and last) AAU title in 440 yd (400 m) in 1965. After that, he retired from sports to work as the AAU track and field administrator from 1965-1972. He was an Executive Director of the AAU from 1970-1980 and Executive Director of USA Track and Field from 19801997. He also was a founding member of the International Athletics Foundation that was created in 1988 and served as vice-president of the International Amateur Athletics Foundation (IAAF) from 1976-1986. Currently, he serves as an adjunct professor for Olympic Sports history at the University of Indianapolis and is the president of the Indiana Olympian Association.

- **Thomas and Julius Jones**—Big Stone Gap, Virginia natives Thomas and Julius Jones were born into a coal-mining family. Their parents worked in the mines to support the family of seven. By the time both men left Big Stone Gap to attend elite universities, they were already hometown football stars. Following successful college careers they were drafted into the NFL. Thomas was later traded to the Chicago Bears and his efforts helped lead the team all the way to the Super Bowl in 2007.

- **Heath Miller,** a Sword's Creek, Virginia native and football star at Honaker High School, graduated from the University of Virginia and signed with the Pittsburgh Steelers in 2005. In 2006 and 2009, he helped to lead the Pittsburgh Steelers to Super Bowl victory.

CHAPTER 2

Successful Writers

Imagination is the key to all of a person's achievements, the mainspring of all human endeavor, the secret door to the soul of a person. Imagination is the workshop of the human mind . . . a creative faculty embracing poetic, artistic, philosophical, scientific, and ethical imagination. —NAPOLEON HILL

Above all, Napoleon Hill was a wordsmith, beginning his writing career at age thirteen as a small-town newspaper reporter with a typewriter he was given by his step-mother. He went on to write countless articles and 13 motivational books. His third book, *Think and Grow Rich*, remains a bestseller. Though Hill wrote nonfiction, he believed in imagination and creativity as fundamental tools toward achieving success and transcending all barriers. It may be argued that Appalachia has drawn national attention primarily as a result of its bestselling and award-winning writers, actors, musicians, and visual artists. Their work has been translated into hundreds of languages and interpreted on both stage and screen in theatres, on Broadway and beyond. Artists like those profiled here continue to credit their hometown values and Hill's principles for their success.

LEE SMITH
Award-Winning Appalachian Author

In 2001, Grundy native and Appalachian author Lee Smith (who now makes her home in North Carolina) published an essay in the *Washington Post* about an event she calls "the Appalachianization of America." Though she was raised to believe that culture was to be found in other places and she would later be sent away to school to find it, Smith writes that her inspiration still springs from her mountain roots. She describes Grammy-award winning bluegrass musician Ralph Stanley's performance at Carnegie Hall following the success of the film *Oh Brother, Where Art Thou?* as symbolic of the irony of Appalachians going somewhere else to find culture. Appalachian culture, she says, found its way to a famed hall in New York City, a culture Smith describes "as rich and as diverse in terms of history, arts, crafts, literature folklore, and music, for instance, as any area in this country."*

Lee Smith's award-winning writing has certainly contributed to that richness of literary culture. Her first book, *The Last Day the Dogbushes Bloomed*, was published shortly after she graduated from Hollins College. Since then, Smith has published nine more novels, four short story collections, several articles, and an oral history project in collaboration with

---

* "Mountain Music's Moment in the Sun: At Last, Appalachia Can Share What It's Always Embraced." *The Washington Post.* Sunday, August 21, 2001: G1.

the students of Grundy High School. Her work has also been immortalized in a touring musical titled *Good Ol' Girls*.

While Smith has found success as a writer, she is generous with gifts of time and help to those who want to follow in her footsteps. She is well-known for her willingness to encourage fledgling writers, even 'discovering' a few Appalachian writers who have gone on to achieve their own success.

How do you define success?

I would define success as living a life that I can feel good about and doing work that I can be proud of. My feelings have more to do with my love for family and friends, my sense of community, and my own private artistic vision than with any kind of outside recognition.

What obstacles, if any, were presented by your region, gender, ethnicity, age, class or other trait(s)?

I don't think any obstacles were presented when I was growing up—or, if they were, I was too ignorant to notice them! It always seemed to me that Grundy was a remarkably egalitarian community; I believe its isolation made people closer and more helpful to each other than in other places. My father always said that they were 'the best people in the world,' and this has always seemed to be the truth. For a kid, the big differences were whether you lived right in town or up one of the hollers, and what church you went to.

If I had gone to school up north, maybe, or in a very urban setting, I might have felt 'looked down upon,' due to my background and Appalachian accent, but I honestly didn't feel this way . . . And as a young writer, I soon realized that it was an advantage to have such different experiences to draw upon. So, I've always felt lucky to be from the Appalachian region where I heard all the best stories I would ever hear (and I'm still hearing them).

What was the burning desire that led you to follow this path, and what was your plan once you determined your purpose?
My writing was not so much a 'burning desire' as an absolute necessity. It was all I wanted to do, it was all I had ever wanted to do, and it was the only thing I was 'good at.' It engaged me more, on every level, than any other activity in the world. This was true when I was twelve years old and it is still true fifty years later. It has been not so much an ambition as an obsession.

The question has always been: How could I live the rest of my life so that I could continue to write? I realized, early on, that nobody can ever count on making a living from writing. The answer has involved many kinds of day jobs.

It is also hard to combine writing with having children, and when my boys were little, I simply didn't write, or I wrote very little, jotting down ideas for future stories on little pieces of paper and jamming them into my jeans pockets for future reference. Especially now that my son, Josh, has died, I am so glad that I put time into the children. It's true that those years are gone before you know it and you can never get them back.

Who were the people allied with you in helping you to become successful?
Several of my professors from Hollins College had an enormous, life-long effect upon me—especially Louis Rubin, one of my first writing teachers and still a close friend. Consequently,

as a teacher, I have tried very hard to pass it on, continuing to try to help my students long after they have left my class. And I have had some amazing students: Appalachian authors Silas House and Pam Duncan among them. I have always had a strong desire to help people, as people have helped me.

At Hollins College, I fell in among a group of friends who were as crazy about writing—and as drunk on literature—as I was. We gave each other a lot of support, and still do. These remarkable women include Pulitzer-prize winning poet Annie Dillard, professors and writers Lucinda MacKethan, Anne Bradford, Anne Jones, writer and reporter Nancy Beckham Ferris, editor Shannon Ravenel, poets Roseanne Coggeshall and Margaret Gibson, and many others.

I married a poet myself . . . about five minutes after we graduated. James Seay was then teaching at Virginia Military Institute. Though this marriage ended in divorce after twelve years, it certainly kept me involved with writing. Now, my husband Hal Crowther, a journalist and essayist, is a great source of support to me in my writing. He has broadened my areas of interest a great deal, as well.

Writing is a paradox; though it requires a great deal of time spent alone, it's also hard to write in total isolation from the world of writers and writing. That's why things like, say, summer writing workshops are so valuable, just so writers can meet and talk to each other.

Which traits do you believe to be the most significant in achieving success?

Irony seems essential to me, along with flexibility and a sense of humor. You have to be serious about your work and your values, but at the same time, you can't take *yourself* too seriously. And you have to remain open to new ideas, people, and the possibilities life presents.

How do you stay focused on your goals?

I don't have a problem staying focused on a goal, if you mean writing. I'd rather write than anything. It's a matter of arranging the rest of my life in order to do it, and frankly, sometimes this cannot be done. Real life is more important.

What is your method for reasoning through a problem or decision?

I have finally learned to let it wait a little. My first decision is often the wrong decision. Sometimes things work themselves out, and you don't have to act, or make any decision at all. Patience is very important.

How have you learned from adversity or defeat?

Like everybody, I have gone through many times of difficulty and defeat. My divorce was hard, for instance, but in the end it was extremely positive for me. I learned that I could stand on my own two feet, handle money, make decisions, get jobs, and take care of my children myself. Several periods of bereavement, disappointment, rejection, and illness have also been very hard.

But the hardest thing in my personal life so far has been my son Josh's long, devastating illness (schizophrenia), its onset at 17, and his recent sudden death at 34 from a heart attack brought on by complications from the illness. This loss has been devastating. I feel so lucky to have had him at all, however, and his own courage in facing his illness is an example for me now. My writing has been a help to me through all times of personal crisis, a sustaining and nourishing thing. Somehow, putting words down on paper in any order at all is a help when the world seems uncontrollable and chaotic.

What do you do for inspiration?
I believe that inspiration may be mostly a 'habit of being,' to use Flannery O' Conner's phrase. We need to look, to listen, to be open to the world's endless variety and its endless gifts.

I believe that inspiration may be mostly a 'habit of being,' to use Flannery O' Conner's phrase. We need to look, to listen, to be open to the world's endless variety and its endless gifts.

ADRIANA TRIGIANI
Bestselling Novelist and Screenwriter

Adriana Trigiani grew up in Big Stone Gap, Virginia in the 1970's. Her hometown and Italian roots proved to be the inspiration for four bestselling novels known as the Big Stone Gap series: *Big Stone Gap, Big Cherry Holler, Milk Glass Moon, and Return to Big Stone Gap*, in addition to six additional novels and two works of nonfiction about her family. Adriana has lived in New York City for most of her adulthood, writing for television shows such as *The Cosby Show* and *A Different World*. Like Lee Smith, she is known for her willingness to help other writers and she remains devoted to her beloved hometown.

How do you define success and what do you count as your greatest accomplishment?

Success is a feeling of buoyancy and hope. It's particularly sweet when work, home and community (friendship) are churning along beautifully and in sync. My greatest accomplishment is living the life I imagined, yet knowing that I'm always a work in progress, an artist who creates.

What obstacles have you encountered and how did you use them in your journey to success?

I'm not a person who dwells on what I didn't get, who got more, or why not me? Those questions are best answered by philosophers and I'm not one. I have noticed that the things I felt might hold me back are the exact things that led me to fulfill a dream or two. I have always been optimistic: it's my nature, and if I fight it, I'm inauthentic. So, I never listened to or surrounded myself with nay-sayers. Sometimes my pep is over the top, but I've learned that energy and drive are gifts, too.

You are well-known for your writing, particularly the Big Stone Gap novels. What was the burning desire that led you to follow your dream, and who were the people allied with you in helping you to become successful?

The burning desire for me has always been to tell a good story. Once I knew that I wanted to tell stories in the theatre (writing plays), for film and television, I set about to work with the best people I could find who would hire me. I have learned all the important things about my work from mentors who took the time to show me the way.

So, the first thing is to be open to those who are experienced and wise. Listen and learn from them. Secondly, be true to your message—to your voice—and the way you believe things should be done. Thirdly, I felt that to make it in the arts I had to live in a mecca for the arts, and for me that is glorious New York City. Surroundings are important—they should be the backdrop of our dreams—and I chose carefully, and then threw myself into the life.

How did you cultivate relationships that would enable you to achieve your goals?

I have been very lucky. Sister Theresa Kelly of the Salesian order encouraged my art. I had great public school teachers in Wise County, Virginia, diligent and caring librarians, and terrific college professors. Once I moved to New York, I worked with spectacular directors and producers who helped me. Ruth Goetz (who wrote *The Heiress* with husband, Augustus) gave me free playwriting lessons for years. Susan Fales-Hill hired me on my first television show, *A Different World*. Of course, the business people were smart and encouraging. My fellow artists have nurtured and encouraged me, particularly Michael Patrick King. Friendships, professional and personal, are crucial to a happy life. I seek counsel daily—sometimes a few times in one day! Friends are the mirrors of your world. They reflect your values, goals, and know your heart's desire.

If I had to boil it down to one thing that gave me a leg up in this world, it would be that both of my parents were college graduates. Their example really set the tone in our home to explore, to travel, and to learn.

What traits do you believe are the most significant in achieving success?

I would choose sense of humor as the most important quality. When I was young, I wanted to be beautiful, but now I know that beauty is not only fleeting, it is highly subjective. Somehow, though, humor crosses all lines: language, social strata, education, you name it. Funny is funny. Of all of the things that I am, this is the gift that I am least responsible for, but most thrilled that I received.

How have you used the power of faith to achieve success?

I've always believed in the unseen. I'm always aware that I'm a spirit first and that any person I deal with is a spirit, also. Souls are perfect and everlasting. When someone is sick or dying, I remind them that they are perfect and limitless, and I give thanks for the gift of that knowledge every day. Faith is everything; there is no private jet, yacht, facelift or diamond ring that can bring you peace. They can bring you acclaim or notice, but not that river of inner peace that comes from wisdom.

How do you "go the extra mile"?

I work constantly. I have had to learn to step back because I always hear a clock ticking, and I'm afraid that this glorious experience of life will be over and I will not have reached my potential. Going the extra mile means no vacations, very little downtime, and a determination to see a project to its final stages. I've learned that solitude, quiet and rest are as important as working hard. This was a big lesson for me, and I'm still learning it.

What motivates and inspires you?

I am motivated by my readers. I want to surprise them, reach them, and relate to them. This drives me to try and write a great line, then a great paragraph, then chapter, and a book. It's always the same: serve my audience.

I get ideas from the smallest things. Sometimes it's the way a brick looks in the streetlight, or the line of a wool coat on a woman walking down the street, or something someone says that catches my ear. It's always small.

How do you maintain a positive attitude, and how do you keep from getting distracted?

I'm usually upbeat and positive. It's natural to me until a machine breaks, and then I stand and fume. I do have to take a breath when confronted with bitterness, anger, and 'poor me' attitudes. I find those emotional states a waste of time. Anger is natural, but work through it and move on. Grudges are poison. Bitterness ruins people. I've seen such talent in people— far more than I'll ever dream of—and they're angry and it kills the spark.

As for distractions, family life and motherhood are the penultimate fabulous distractions. That has been a hard adjustment for me. I'm a bit of a monk, and that's over now that I have a daughter and husband. However, I never let a good time get in the way of my work. I love a party, but I always go to bed early and get up early and work. My friends laugh at me sometimes, but if I'm not happy with my work, I'm not much good elsewhere.

How do you reason through decisions or problems?
I sit down in a quiet place and write down all the negatives and all of the positives of a dilemma. (My mother taught me this.) Then, I reason through the lists. Then, I pray about it. I ask a confidante their opinion . . . and I truly listen.

When have you learned from failure or defeat?
I fail all the time! I can't list one major defeat, but I've experienced them all. I've been fired, broke, sad, grief-stricken, cheated on, and lied to. But failure, in its own way, is necessary. Without failure, we would never change. One thing life is all about is the ability to change, to let go, and to move forward. So, I guess I should give thanks for failure.

Failure, in its own way, is necessary. Without failure, we would never change. One thing life is all about is the ability to change, to let go, and to move forward.

How do you budget your time and money?
Time well spent comes when you're doing the right job for you. Suddenly, you have enough time because you are passionate about using it as a means to an end. So, it flows naturally from doing what you're supposed to be doing with your life. I only have one philosophy about money, and that is to spend it. Save and be responsible, but invest in you: travel, take classes, live where you want to live. Put your investment in you and then, I have found, the money flows to provide you with what you need and enough to assist those around you.

Can you talk about environment and success?
If you choose to live in New York City, it means you thrive on excitement. Every morning that I wake up in this city is a good one, because I'm in the place that nourishes my soul, feeds my intellect, and keeps me moving. Your environment is the backdrop of your actions, and if it is less than inspiring, there's an immediate problem. Everything in your life should be beautiful and functional and speak to you. Meaning comes from surrounding yourself with joy . . . and that includes the wallpaper.

Hill Country Artists

- **Don Whitehead** was born on April 28, 1908, in the coal camp of Inman, Virginia, and his family moved to Harlan, Kentucky during his childhood. When he was only ten years old, Whitehead published his first news story for the local newspaper about a murder that he had witnessed. Whitehead worked for the Lafollette Press and became city editor of the *Harlan Daily Enterprise*, covering the 1930s Harlan County labor wars. He began work as a reporter for the *Knoxville Journal* in 1934, and one year later he joined the Associated Press as a night editor in Memphis. Just before the United States' involvement in World War II, Whitehead's feature writing led to a job at the AP's New York Bureau. In 1942, the AP sent him to Egypt, where he was assigned to the British Eighth Army as it began its campaign against Rommell's Africa Corp. Whitehead landed on Omaha Beach on D-Day, June 6, 1944 with the First Infantry Division's 16th Regiment. He covered the fighting on the beachhead, the breakout at St. Lo, and the sweep across France. During World War II, Whitehead earned the nickname "Beachhead Don" because he was present at no fewer than five Allied landings. He was awarded the Medal of Freedom by President Truman. In July, 1950 he was sent to cover the Korean War where he distinguished himself as one of the leading journalists in the field; he was awarded the Pulitzer Prize a year later, followed by the George Polk Memorial Award for wire service reporting. In 1952, Whitehead won *another* Pulitzer Prize for his international reporting on a secret fact-finding trip to Korea taken by President-elect Eisenhower. Whitehead went on to write six books including the best selling *The FBI Story*, a history of the FBI from 1908 to 1955.

- **George C. Scott** is a Wise County, Virginia native, like Napoleon Hill. Following his mother's death just before his eighth birthday, he was raised by his father, an executive at the Buick Motor Company. After a four-year career with the Marines beginning in 1945, Scott enrolled in journalism classes at the University of Missouri, where he fell in love with acting. His role in "Richard III" in New York City got the attention of critics in the late 1950's. He began working in television, mostly in live broadcasts of plays, and in 1959 he won the part of the crafty prosecutor in *Anatomy of a Murder*. This role led Scott to his first Oscar nomination for Best Supporting Actor. He won the Best Actor Oscar in 1970 for his portrayal of General Patton in *Patton*. He is also well-known for his portrayal of Ebenezer Scrooge in the 1984 film adaptation of the Dickens classic *A Christmas Carol*. In all, Scott was nominated for 19 awards and won a total of eleven critical awards for his work.

- **Carter and Ralph Stanley** were born and raised in Dickenson County, Virginia, the sons of farmers. Their musical interests were influenced at an early age by the Monroe Brothers and Mainer's Mountaineers by way of the Grand Ole Opry radio show. Their band, the Clinch Mountain Boys, began performing in 1946, and they are credited with being the first band devoted to the musical style of bluegrass, created by Bill Monroe in the mid1940's. (Ralph prefers the term "mountain music.") Carter sang lead and played guitar and Ralph sang tenor, accompanied by his banjo. The brothers wrote many of their own songs; Carter had a particular knack for writing simple lyrics that portrayed strong emotion. The Stanleys' style can best be described as a traditional 'mountain soul' sound that remained close to the Primitive Baptist vocal style they learned from their parents and others near their southwestern Virginia home. Carter Stanley, who passed away in 1966 is credited as one of the greatest singers in the history of country music.

  Dr. Ralph Stanley, who was awarded an honorary doctorate in music from Lincoln Memorial University in 1976, is an icon among country music fans, and his popularity has spread into popular culture, as well. His haunting voice could be heard in the 2000 film *Oh Brother, Where Art Thou?* earning him a Grammy (he has been awarded several of them over the course of his musical career.) The Stanley Brothers were inducted into the International Bluegrass Music Hall of Honor in 1992. In 2006, President George W. Bush awarded Dr. Stanley the National Medal of Arts, the nation's highest honor for artistic excellence.

- **Verna Mae Slone** was born in Knott County, Kentucky in 1914 where she and her husband raised five sons. What is notable about Slone (besides the body of work that she contributed to

Appalachian literature) is that she was already in her sixties when she began publishing her writing about Appalachia, writing that was inspired by her love of the mountains and her dedication to an authentic representation of mountain culture and people. Though her work was originally intended for her grandchildren, she accrued a wide audience, earning glowing reviews for her book *What My Heart Wants to Tell* from the *New York Times* and *Christian Science Monitor.* Other works include *How We Talked, Common Folks, Sarah Ellen* and *Rennie's Way.*

- **Jean Ritchie** is a balladeer and songwriter who was born in Viper, Kentucky. Credited for popularizing the melodies of the fretted dulcimer, Ritchie is cited as a notable member of the 1950's and 60's folk revival. Her recording career began at Elektra Records in 1950; she went on to record over forty albums that included ballads, folk songs and original works. Songs such as "Black Waters" illustrate her social and environmental activism. She has published ten books, including the autobiography *Singing Family of the Cumberlands.*

- **Loretta Lynn** is a Grammy award-winning singer/songwriter from Butcher Hollow, Kentucky whose life was immortalized in the 1980 Oscar-winning film *Coal Miner's Daughter,* which was based on Lynn's 1976 autobiography. Lynn was married at thirteen and the mother of four children by age seventeen. She was discovered in 1960 and would blaze a trail for women in country music for the next fifty years. Lynn's music has led to countless awards but she is perhaps best known for being one of the first country music singers whose songs examined topics such as adultery and birth control from a feminist perspective.

CHAPTER 3

Success in Business

When you train your mind to seek out opportunities, you will find that every day literally presents you with more opportunities than you can take advantage of. —NAPOLEON HILL

The word "success" is most frequently associated with the field of business, where achievement is equated with profit. At the time of this writing, however, the global economy is teetering on the brink of recession and the business world has experienced the most difficult period of instability since the Great Depression. Joblessness and home foreclosures are at record highs. The outlook is bleak for college graduates with high hopes and crisp new diplomas. While entrepreneurship is always a gamble, the peaks and valleys that accompany profit ventures are certain.

The entrepreneurs in these pages achieved success in spite of such difficulty, refusing to wait until the time was "right." Napoleon Hill, whose success as a motivational writer and speaker occurred in similarly bleak times during the Great Depression, knew the bitterness of failure all too well. He would point to those principles that work consistently through periods of upheaval.

DR. J. CHARLES SMIDDY
Vice-President, Consumer Product Sales, White Lily, Inc. (1952–1995)
President And CEO Of S.N.S. Enterprises Inc.
President And CEO of C-N-E Enterprises

Dr. Charles Smiddy began his career in business at the tender age of eight. Following his service during WWII, Smiddy gained experience in the grocery business before joining White Lily Foods, where he worked for 43 years. Following his retirement, Smiddy embarked on a second career as President and CEO of two companies, when most people would be settling into a life of relaxation and travel. He was recognized with an honorary doctorate in business administration from the University of the Cumberlands. Though Dr. Smiddy passed away in 2010, several years after giving this interview, he left his mark in a field where he seemed destined to succeed.

In Charles Smiddy's words . . .

A Start-Up Business from Papers and Popcorn

I started out very young. My older brother and I couldn't get a paper route because of our age. So we wrote to the *Cincinnati Post*, because they had no business in Williamsburg, Kentucky. If we ordered twenty-five papers, and we didn't sell them all, we could cut the top off and get credit for a penny and a half (that's what they cost us.) I found out real quick that there were more people coming from Ohio, right through the middle of town on 25W going to Florida. I began holding up the paper and yelling, 'Cincinnati Post!' and they stopped, backed up, and got a paper!

I was eight years old and my brother was close to ten when we made enough money to buy us a Ranger bicycle with a luggage carrier and a light. My uncle and aunt came in from Chicago, and they wanted to take us back to Chicago with them for the summer. Of course, Mother and Daddy weren't about to let us both go, so they let us draw straws. I won the trip. My brother, Jim, said, 'Charles, if you'll let me go to Chicago I'll give you my part of the bicycle.' So I said, 'You've got a deal.' So he went to Chicago, and I finished delivering the papers.

I was down on the courthouse square selling those papers and there was a guy with a popcorn machine. He started looking over the bicycle and said, 'I believe I've got a motor that'll fit on there. How can we trade?'

I said, 'What is that you've got there?'

He said, 'A popcorn machine.' He gave me five dollars for food, and traded that popcorn machine for the bicycle. Well, I was in business!

I took it home, where my mother helped me clean and shine it up. I painted it silver. We had a grocery store in Jellico, and a sign painter showed me how to put a sign on it. I began selling popcorn and it's amazing at the money that I was taking in.

So, I had this popcorn business on the courthouse square. People were coming and going all the time. When business was slow, I'd go down to the jailhouse, the beauty shop and to the garages and take orders. I'd go back and pop it for them

and take it to them fresh, and they'd say, 'Put a lot of oil on it.'
I used Wesson oil.

The first big day of business was an all-day singing which
they held once a year. I had a half a year's supply of popcorn
at a nickel a bag. By one or two o'clock, I was sold out of every
bit and had so many nickels in my pocket that they rubbed my
legs raw. I jumped the price on my paper, *The Cincinnati Post*,
because it was so much in demand that they couldn't get it
anyplace else. Sometimes I'd sell it for a dime! That was pretty
good money.

Faulkner, the jailer of the town, bought his daughter a
brand new bicycle. Somebody ran over it and broke the wheel.
So, I offered to buy it, and he let me have that bicycle for five
dollars. I took it down to a friend of mine that had a garage and
he straightened the wheels up. So I had a bicycle, and a popcorn machine, and the paper and I was doing good business!

The man who had bought my Ranger bicycle came back
and said, 'I can't get that motor in between those bars. How
can we trade?' Of course, the girl's bicycle doesn't have that
bar, so I said, 'I'll trade with you for five dollars.' He gave me
five dollars and that Ranger bicycle, so I had my bicycle back
where I started, and this was in about five weeks. That was
about 1936. I was ten.

I bought more bicycles and I rented them when the country boys came to town. Every now and then, some of them
would ride on home. I'd find out where they were, and contact my mother's uncle, who was the sheriff. He'd say, 'Son,
we'll just go down there and get it!' He said, 'Now, I'll tell you
what. You can tell them that you won't prosecute them if they
give you $25.' So, I got $25 for not prosecuting them, and I'd

get my bicycle back. I learned how to trade with some of the experts around.

A Soldier's Eye for Business

WWII broke out and as soon as I was eighteen years old, I joined the Marine Corps. We flew to Guam on a C-47, a transporter. We had to put the long-range fuel tanks in there to get over the water. We were flying mail to all these different islands in the South Pacific, especially Okinawa.

Every time you'd land someplace you'd have to have cigarettes, which we hid in parachutes. We bought them from the Navy for $50 a case and sold them for $400 a case. I'd also buy those beautiful silk kimonos and pajamas and take them back to Guam where those boys would send them to their girlfriends. I'd sell some of them for $50. I don't know what the boys were telling their girlfriends but *I* was making money.

I wrote a few letters while I was over there. I never will forget this boy from the Bronx. When I was in Guam on the weekend I'd need a Jeep, and he'd get me one, so I'd answer his letters for him. I practically had him married! One time I was gone away, and when I came back, he was in desperate need of me answering some letters for him! So I sat down and I thought a little while and I wrote down just what I told him:

I received your letter in due time, but regardless of the agitated anticipation I had for reading it, I allowed it to remain dormant for [whatever time it was] and I decided to reply.

It was silly but it was fun. They could read and write but just couldn't express themselves. I would write it pretty fancy for them and included maps and stuff like that. I made it a point to be a little different.

Looking Through a "Window" of Opportunity

When I got out of the service, I had quite a few opportunities. I never drew enough pay to live on, so I'd pick out a store that had dirty windows and I'd say, 'How'd you like me to change this window for you? You need to clean it up.' The store owners had no people coming in there saying that. This was around Christmastime and I'd find four or five windows. I'd clean the windows, find empty boxes, and take cotton and I'd sprinkle it with silver. I could decorate with crepe paper because I'd learned how to do that working at a drugstore. I could take that crepe paper and make it pretty. I'd say, 'Pay me what you want to pay me,' and they'd always pay me more! That was the strategy. If I had asked for $50 or $100 they would have hesitated, but once they'd see what I had done, they would always pay me more.

My daddy had a grocery store in Jellico and he wanted me to come and work for him. The store business just wasn't fast enough for me and I didn't like running the credit. I'll never forget a woman who came in and said, 'Well, I can't pay you today; I don't know when I can pay.' I told my daddy I couldn't be in this business.

"From Scratch to the Top in Two Years' Time"

I ran into Mr. Renfro of the Renfro Supply Company at the bank and asked him if he needed a good salesman. He said he needed a lot of good salesmen. I said, 'I'd like to have a job selling groceries. I know all about groceries. I was raised in a grocery store.' So, he wrote me a letter and told me to come and talk to him. He said he didn't have anything open, but he wanted me to learn the business. He had building supplies, wholesale groceries, and auto supplies.

I told Mr. Renfro I could open up a territory. I went on the road and I didn't have one customer. He agreed to pay me $200 a month for two months and he furnished my gas. There I was: a new baby at my house, the money to pay the difference in my car, and a territory without a customer! I just found out where they were going. I started at Pineville, Kentucky and worked right down through Middlesboro, Kentucky to Powell Valley, Virginia. I figured out that I could make a living right down that valley.

During the war, no one could get field fencing, metal roofing, or sheet rock, but I had it and I was working on commission. I left before daylight and came back after dark. I'd see somebody starting to build a house, I'd go out there and make a pretty good sale. That's how I built a good relationship with the store. I'd sell the roofing by figuring out how much he could take on his house and go back to the store and make the deal. I sold plenty of field fence and barbed wire.

I started to work without one customer and in 1951 I was the top salesman. They've got my picture in a little book, titled *Renfro Revelations*. He'd put this book out every month. Of course, the first year, I got a bonus, and I was really in business. That was going from scratch to the top in two years' time, but I had to *work*.

A Poetic Grocery Salesman

Customers would stand around the store to hear what I was going to say next. I could make a broom stand right up in the floor, and I'd say, 'Women love it because it's so well-balanced!' I'd sell a dozen brooms about every stop I made.

The next time I'd carry shoe polish. I'd shine up one shoe and leave the other one as dirty as it could be.

You've got to find the need and then find a way to supply it. There's no use in going into an area that does not have electricity and try to sell light bulbs.

Working for White Lily Foods

White Lily came to me and offered me a job. I took the job while living in Williamsburg, KY and my territory was in Harlan and Appalachia, VA at the wholesale house. After that, they wanted me to work the territory in Jellico until they hired another salesman. I was doing more business in both territories than they had been doing in the past. I began holding store sales. I could auction, so they bought me a public address system. I got a little oven and I started baking biscuits. I got that idea from Harland Sanders.

Harland Sanders (founder of KFC) had a restaurant but he wasn't doing a lot of business. Behind his restaurant he had a carport. In the summer, he'd be back there in the back with a tub. He'd buy from me eight bags of what we called 'cut-off' flour (which was cheaper) and four bags of White Lily flour. He would put that in a tub and mix it with his herbs. He had a hand-fan with his picture on it, wearing that Kentucky Colonel bow-tie.

I found out that his was a serious business when a friend sent me one of these hand fans with his picture on it. After that, I paid attention to Harland Sanders, who got into the franchising business in a big way. But he didn't make the money out of it that John Y. Brown, [Jr.]* did.

I began holding store sales. We gave away a plate and other things with a bag of flour. I held store sales all around *by request.* They remodeled the A & P store in Harlan, KY, which was the largest volume store they had. They had a big grand opening, where I was on the public address system. I could get the salesmen to give me anything I wanted. I could get as many sausages as I wanted if I'd serve them up with my biscuits.

I'd get on the public address system and I'd say, 'If there's anybody in the checkout lane with a bag of White Lily flour, we're going to give you this.' Sometimes I'd give them a loaf of bread, for example. I'd watch, and if I saw somebody going through the checkout lane that didn't have White Lily flour and they had something else, then that's when I'd offer to give them something big and they'd want to take the flour back and swap it!

Becoming a Broker

I announced to the company one day that I was going into the brokerage business. I felt like I could get the accounts and I could sell. The first account that I got was Smucker's Jelly Pre-

---

* Colonel Sanders sold his company, which he began at age 65, for $2 million to John Y. Brown and other investors. They later sold the company, which had grown to 3,500 franchises, for $285 million (KFC corporation's official web site.)

serves. Cas Walker* was a good friend of mine and I'd done these store sales for him, so he helped me. He had this Supermarket Institute. All the supermarkets belonged to it and they'd go out to Chicago and get different ideas from companies that would have items on display. At the institute, he'd see a product and say, 'I believe I could sell that. You ought to talk to Smiddy,' and I'd come along behind him and give the company a card. They didn't have to come to me; I was already there.

I picked up Del Monte Foods, Bird's Eye Frozen Foods, and United Bean Company. I sat down and made a list of what I needed: dried beans for this part of the country, potted meat like Vienna sausages, canned vegetables, canned fruits, and fish—salmon, mackerel, sardines.

I made some people mad because I was taking their accounts. You run the risk of being considered unethical because you're not supposed to ask for other people's accounts, but if a company wanted to change over, I was the man. I got into that business pretty fast. I had the whole market stirred up.

Selling with Ferris Wheels

I had a friend named Walt who had a playground near Oak Ridge that included a Ferris wheel. He couldn't run it in the winter, so business was slow. I said we could take that Ferris wheel over to Kingsport, Tennessee, where I had a friend who ran Oakwood Markets. We could put it on that parking lot. I

---

* Cas Walker, born in Sevier County, Tennessee was a popular politician and grocery store entrepreneur. He invested in a Knoxville grocery store in 1924, and turned the store into a successful chain. Walker was also a popular radio and television host who launched the careers of the Everly Brothers and twelve-year-old Dolly Parton.

said, 'Customers can get a free ticket to ride that Ferris wheel with each item that I'm selling. You could run it all day and into the night and if they don't have a ticket, they can pay you to ride.' He sold a lot of tickets to ride, the stores got a good promotion, and I got all these sales for nothing!

I was doing so well in the brokerage business that it was moving too fast. White Lily talked me into coming back to work for them and they made me a good offer. They had put in a retirement plan while I was gone, and you had to be there three years before you could participate in that plan. I said, 'I was with you ten years before I left and went into the brokerage business.' I thought long-term and where I was going to go.

They came to me with another offer: they would agree for me to participate in the pension fund at once. They wanted me to open up new territory and train new salesmen. They gave me the title of Merchandising Manager and the authority to go to any district. I'd just show up to see if they were working and what they were doing.

Climbing the Ladder of Success Through Personal Initiative

We had exclusive relationships with stores everywhere. From the day I started working, I had a different idea about how to hire and train a sales force and what I wanted them to do. I didn't want a guy with a college degree because all he wanted to do was carry a briefcase. What I wanted them to do was to make those calls, build those displays, set those stores up, and network with the store managers. I would go to a sales meeting, and show them how to set it up. We conducted a study of what a woman does when she goes to a supermarket. I'll tell you one thing she won't do: she won't bend down any more than she has to, and she won't reach up over her head any more than she has to. What she wants to do is buy at eye level. Your percentage of sales when you're merchandising is based on shelf space and getting them at eye level.

I wanted the salespeople to look sharp, and when they drove up to the front of a store—I don't care how big it was—I wanted that car to shine. I didn't want a bunch of junk in it. I inspected their cars. I did a lot of things you couldn't get away with now. Someone came in for an interview one time, and he had on white socks, and I said, 'We don't need him unless he changes those socks!' I became Senior Vice-President and Director of Sales.

The Griffin Report showed the top-selling items in cities like Atlanta and list the share of markets. White Lily Flour became the number one item sold on the Atlanta market. When I left the company, we had a 63% share of the market on flour, and we had a 46% share on corn meal. I'd send a salesman in to a store to say, 'You've got a lot of dead space and what you need to do is let me reset it. We have a heavy share of market.' So we had the biggest percentage of shelf space.

I took a piece of paper and put that in the floor [to illustrate how much space it would take to stack] flour in a 25-bale display and a 50-bale display. That would sell displays. If the store manager put it on display they'd give you a better price, and the more you'd sell, the better share of the market you were getting all the time. When our market share got up to 40 or 50%, my tactic was to explain to the manager that the store would increase its business if they would feature White Lily.

I left White Lily in 1995 at 69. I went through seven presidents, and every time they'd come to me and they'd say, 'We want you to stay. If you make the numbers, we'll give you a big bonus.' We were doing it honestly and we were making the numbers.

Learning the Business of Land

I got into the land business out of my hip pocket on a used envelope. I bought some apartments in Atlanta around 1971, when things were tight and foreclosures were coming up. Before I sold them, I bought everything around them. I bought the apartment buildings for $175,000, and paid $50,000 down. The first thing I did was clean them up and raise the price of the rent, and it paid for itself. Then I started buying the property around it. I sold this property for $70 a square foot which gives you $3,470,000. That's high-priced land. So every time I sold something, I bought something.

Advice for Today's Entrepreneurs.

My advice for young people today is to get into something that you really like. I can truthfully say that every day I went to work I was enthused. If you're happy at what you're doing, you're going to be successful at it. If you do make some money, don't run out and spend it. Get yourself a little nest egg. I have made some big deals, and the only time I ever went to the bank was when I bought my first house with a G.I. loan. I paid that loan off in a year because I moved. I made a profit on it, and I took that profit and picked up a house and borrowed the remainder of that, and that's all the money I ever borrowed from the bank. A lot of people think that's the way to go, but you should get yourself into a situation to where you can pay cash down. People now will dig themselves a hole they can't get out of. You may have to work a little extra and you have to do without a few things, but get a little nest egg.

I can truthfully say that every day I went to work I was enthused. If you're happy at what you're doing, you're going to be successful at it.

PAL BARGER,
Entrepreneur Founder Of Pal's Sudden Service

Fred "Pal" Barger, Jr. opened his first Pal's Sudden Service restaurant in Kingsport, Tennessee in 1956. Barger's savvy business practices led to a chain of restaurants throughout the region. His is the only restaurant to receive the prestigious Malcolm Baldridge National Quality Award and two Tennessee Excellence Awards. Barger's practices gained so much global attention that he established the Business Excellence Institute in 2000 which attracts business managers and owners, as well as leaders of non-profit organizations, from all over the world to learn what makes Barger so successful.

In Pal Barger's words . . .

My mother and father were in the restaurant business, and I knew that wasn't what I wanted to do. I wanted to be an accountant. I saw a restaurant operation in Austin, Texas called '2J's' in the early 1950's when I was in the Air Force. They had evidently copied the McDonald brothers. (McDonald's started in San Bernadino, California in the 1940's). We'd eat there all the time, and I thought this restaurant was a great idea. You don't have dishes to wash or seating.

I asked if I could come in and see it. They had it glassed in on three sides so you could see what was going on, but they wouldn't let me come inside. So, after work, I would sit in the back of the car with binoculars and watch them. I knew how many people they had working. They had the old-time cash registers where the numbers would pop up, so I'd keep a record of their sales for an hour. I could just about figure out what their food cost was because I had some experience. I decided that was what I wanted to do.

I came back to Tennessee and finished my business degree at East Tennessee State University. About nine months before I finished school, I leased a restaurant in Marion, Virginia, called The Virginia House. It was in connection with a motel there and we served breakfast, lunch, and dinner. I lived in a $50 per month house, and worked from 6:00 a.m. to 10:00 p.m., seven days a week. I saved $10,000 and then I came home and I borrowed $10,000. That's what it cost me to put in the first restaurant. I leased the land and bought the building and equipment for $20,000. The last restaurant we built cost a million.

How do you define success?

I define success as living life where you have good friends and where you work at something you enjoy to produce positive results for your family, friends, community, and business associates.

What was the burning desire that led you to follow your path?
To be the best and to do it with style.

How do you achieve success through teamwork?
The owner/operators will go through about four years of training before they have their own store. We've got about 650 employees. The only people outside the operation are me, my assistant, and Thom Crosby, the President and CEO. When we won the Baldridge Award in 2000, they asked where our secretaries, public relations people, and marketing departments were. We outsource all of that. Creative Energy does our advertising.

Flash cards are used to reinforce the Pals philosophy. Every employee is tested regularly using a box of laminated, color-coded flash cards on topics from "ethics" to "tea brewing." They also use iPods with digital video for training new employees.
If our flash cards need to be redone, we have a team of three operators who get together and do that. This gives you an idea of the depth we go to in training. Most people quit a job because of lack of training. They're embarrassed because they don't know what everybody else knows. We have iPod training, which we just started. They can go out and actually see where they're going to be working. When we open a store, three managers will work each day there for five or six hours. They do that for three weeks. Then Thom and the regular owner/operator will be there. Everyone helps everyone else. Everyone knows how to do the jobs. When we decided to change the

uniforms, there were 69 hourly employees who volunteered to be on that team outside of work. We have cooperation and at some point we have everybody on some kind of team, which benefits their store.

Who were the people allied with you in helping you to become successful?

Thom Crosby, President and CEO, and Tony Barone, who designed the building (on a napkin) have been instrumental in our success. Tony was from Chicago and moved to New York before coming here. He was in the cosmetics business, and he was a restaurant designer and artist. At one time he was recognized as the top restaurant designer in the country. Everyone in the industry admires him. I still communicate with him once a month. I also formed relationships with other people in the restaurant industry.

I have attended restaurant shows in different countries. I'd sit next to people on a six to 24-hour flight. I learned more sitting next to those people and talking to them. You couldn't buy their time outside of that situation. I learned more talking to those people than what I saw on the trips.

Which traits are the most significant in helping to achieve success?

A positive mental attitude, courtesy, frankness of manner and speech, sense of humor, and effective showmanship.

How have you gone the extra mile?

The owner/operator system pays somebody three or four times what you'd ordinarily hire them for. That cuts your income down but you've got to have a place to start to get it to that level.

For the Meadowview Conference Center, the city wanted to impose a two percent restaurant tax to fund it, and put it on the restaurants. So, I spearheaded getting all the restaurants together. When you own a restaurant, you come in contact with a lot of people, so we got petitions together. This went on for about three months or so. We collected 38,000 names against the restaurant tax. I made a lot of enemies. They were picking one segment of the economy to pay for something that everyone is going to benefit from; 67% of tax dollars come from fast food. It took six months out of my life to get the sales tax passed. If you believe in something like that you need to give it 100%.

We raised 3.5 million dollars to build a field house for Dobyns Bennett High School. We encourage all our employees to get involved in the community and we speak to civic clubs and colleges. You've got to do things to help your community.

How do you work with others to achieve your goals?
I think you look for character and personality and then you can train them to do the job if you get somebody with the right attitude.

Describe a time when you learned a valuable lesson from adversity or defeat?
I can't think of an idea that I had that really didn't work. I didn't expand Pal's because before Ronald Reagan took office I was in the 91% tax bracket, which is really no incentive to

expand it. I'll use an example: say I had a business and I was making $150,000. I could draw $50,000 salary and pay 41% tax on it. Then, the other $100,000 I'd make, I'd have to pay a corporate tax on it, which is 50%. So now I'm down to $50,000 in dividends and would have to pay a 41% tax on that. So if I can only keep 9% what's the incentive to expand?

I went to a dinner theatre and watched a show and thought, 'This is a pretty neat concept.' I opened a dinner theatre and ran it for about 13 years—'Old West'. I opened it in 1966, I think. I could travel to New York and see shows, hire directors, put an ad in *Backstage* and hire actors. We could do a show for four weeks, and two weeks into that bring in two more actors.

In what ways has your environment been an influence in your success?

I lived a good life; my parents were good to me. My mom took in sewing for two dollars an hour and my dad drove a buggy for Pet Dairy to deliver milk. In first grade I had one pair of pants and I had to come home and change and let mother wash my pants so I could wear them to school the next day. I didn't know any different; I thought everybody was like that.

To go to a movie for nine cents was a big deal. When I was about twelve years old, Dad had a job at a bonding company and did pretty well. Before that we did a beer delivery. Beer was hard to get during the war, so he got cases of different brands and delivered beer to homes by the case. Dad rented a place for $20 a month and offered pit barbecue, hamburgers, and beer and did a really good business. Then he opened Skoby's Restaurant.

So I've experienced being poor and being wealthy and I like the second better. I think it motivates you to try and be successful; if you grow up with a silver spoon in your mouth you're not as motivated. I've been there and don't want to be there again. I wouldn't change anything. I'm glad I went through that.

In what ways have you used your environment to achieve success?

When we opened the first Pal's, we had a couple of ice cream stores and you'd get out of your car and go to the window. Ours was the only business like that, so people didn't understand the concept of coming up to the window to order their food and taking it back to the car. We had to keep somebody on the lot and explain the concept to them. They'd blow their horns. Some of them would say, 'You need to get some curb hops or you'll go out of business,' and then drive off. It was hard to get people to understand that concept. McDonald's didn't come in until ten or fifteen years later. So we had to educate the customers. We sold hamburgers for 19 cents and French fries for a dime and Cokes for a dime, so at 48 cents and two cents tax you could have lunch.

Do you encounter prejudice when people know that you're from east Tennessee?

No. In fact, we've got people from all over the world here to learn. A lot of people know about the Baldridge Award, and we gain instant respect. We're going for the Tennessee Quality Award and next year, we'll apply for the Baldridge again. A lot of people think once they've won it they don't have to try anymore.

What advice do you give to others who want to follow your example of success?

Develop a positive mental attitude. If you stay positive and upbeat, and if you see the possibilities for success, you will find ways to align yourself to succeed.

WENDELL BARNETTE,
Entrepreneur Founder Of Double Kwik Markets

Wendell Barnette worked his way from humble beginnings to develop the Double Kwik Market chain, a successful series of convenience stores that he sold in 2007. Like Pal Barger, Barnette saw opportunity in another successful business, the 7-Eleven, which inspired him to develop his own multi-million dollar idea. He has also been successful in the real estate and radio business. Barnette currently owns and operates several Ford-Lincoln automobile dealerships throughout the region. While his business experience has garnered financial success, Barnette stays true to simple values of faith, hard work and giving back.

In Wendell Barnette's words . . .

To succeed in business, you have to be in the right place and know the right people. I never sat down and said that I would have 65 convenience stores. I just worked it all out and a lot of good things happened.

I was born in Keokee, Virginia, and then Mom and Pop moved to Guest River; I think I was about three or four years old. Dad was a coal miner. We went to a little schoolhouse in Wise. I have seven sisters and four brothers. We had a farm that we leased from some folks living in Bristol, a couple hundred acres where we raised corn and beans, potatoes, strawberries, cows, pigs, and chickens. (I didn't like working on a farm.) We were poor, but we didn't know it. We had plenty to eat, clothes to wear and we were made to do our chores. We had a lot of friends.

My dad was one of the most honest men I've ever known. He was strong and he worked hard. He didn't have an education, but he was a family man and he would do anything for his family. He died of black lung at 73. My mom is still living, and she's 95; she's the strongest person I've ever known—and still is. She raised twelve kids, she had a tiny store, and she worked in the gardens and fields all the time. I don't know how she did it.

I graduated from J.J. Kelly High School and then went to Clinch Valley College [now University of Virginia's College at Wise.] My business was Double Kwik [convenience stores]. But when I first started working I was in construction. My construction experience was great. I drew the plans and built most of the stores. Actually when I was at Clinch Valley College, I took engineering classes. I didn't want to be an engineer, but I did learn some things that stayed with me. Sometimes opportunities will present themselves, but you have to take advantage of them while they're there or they will pass by. You won't get them all, but you'll get several.

I got married and we had twin boys. I went to Fairfax to get a job with the government. After the first day I didn't like it. Then, I became a brick mason, and learned a lot. I did that for about nine years. On my way to and from work, I would listen to Earl Nightingale, who had a five minute radio segment. [Nightingale credited *Think and Grow Rich* for his success.] I was doing well with construction, but I didn't want to do that forever. I really started listening and started applying principles from Napoleon Hill.

I saw 7-Elevens pop up everywhere. My mom and dad had a grocery store, and I knew that I wanted to do that because I had worked there while I was in school. So I bought their little store. It was just a little Mom and Pop store with a stove in the middle; I paid my mom $15,000 for it. I did a lot of work and then it took off from there. For the first few years, I had a partnership with my brother, Jerry. I bought him out when we had sixteen stores. He didn't like it as well as I did. So I bought his half in 1993. For ten years we made payments to him and by that time we had added 46 more stores.

The rest is history.

I worked with a lot of really good people. At one time we had 68 stores, and then sold off three smaller ones. We made over $200 million in sales. We sold the rest in November, 2007. FasMart made me an offer I couldn't refuse; every time I see a FasMart I just say, 'Thank you.' I worked on selling for about seven years and we got exactly the deal I wanted.

We also buy and sell commercial real estate and I still have several pieces. We have a couple of radio stations. We had a cable TV business. I had my own wholesale that serviced my stores. I bought directly from Phillip Morris, Kraft, and Wise County Tobacco.

I had no idea I was going to be in the radio business, but it was just an opportunity that Don Wax gave me. He started

WAXM. He had lots of good ideas but he never put them to work. He came to my office and said, 'I'm going to sell you my radio station,' to which I replied, 'I don't know if I want a radio station.' I couldn't resist the deal, however, so I bought the station, and I ended up with three radio stations.

The lack of capital was my first obstacle. If I had the money I could have had 500 stores. Banks are tough, but I had good stock in the bank; I was successful there. Another obstacle in business is that you need good help to take care of customers, but you can only pay employees so much while taking care of them and keeping them motivated.

My burning desire has to be good health, good family, and the want to be successful . . . and money isn't a bad thing. You can do a lot of good with some of the money. Just keep applying the principles and looking for opportunities and taking advantage of all the opportunities without going deep into debt. I always kept my debt really low. When I sold out my debt was only five percent of what I received for the stores, which is unheard of. So we tried to not live above our means and we got to do the things we wanted. I tried to have a great relationship with everyone, especially my vendors. Most of them would say that I'd be the only guy who would pay on time, which would help me get better deals. Vendors like Coke and Pepsi were just tremendous to work with. If I needed something they'd help me out. They even helped me find new locations.

A positive attitude has to be the number one trait for success. If you don't have the right attitude then you won't have anything. All of them are important. Sincerity, courtesy, tact, smiling, sense of humor, flexibility. Fondness for people for sure. A good handshake. You need humility. Faith and the sense of justice also stand out. I hope I've exemplified most of those.

I grew up in a Baptist home, and went to church with my mom. I had not read the Bible that much, but I'd been taught well. I was taught the Golden Rule, taught to be honest, taught from the Bible and Commandments and all those things. I ended up praying a lot. I'm not a saint or anything—never pretended to be anything I wasn't—but we'd go to church. It's important to believe in the Supreme Being. Whatever you want, whatever you need, even for those who don't believe pray to Him because there's no one else. Just have faith in God to know that He is there. Try to be good and be good to others, needy folks especially. Most of the time what we would give would be anonymous.

Brenda (my wife) is always doing things for needy folks and most of the time they don't know where it comes from. She's a good person. I probably would not have been nearly as successful without Brenda. She's just always done a little more here and there. I'm a little hotheaded and have a bit of a temper and she calms me down. But our faith has really been strong, and I don't remember when I haven't prayed.

To go the extra mile you can't work eight hours a day. I'd always heard that you need to work twelve hours a day. But most times we ended up working for sixteen hours a day. There was even a period of time when Jerry and I hadn't had a day off in seven years. Doing for others and showing appreciation for what they do to help you is another example. Writing cards is important; they don't know you appreciate them unless you tell them. That takes a bit of time but not much. You need those extra hours figuring out what you need to do the next hour or the next week and set goals. Usually I would set goals for a year and have them accomplished in three months, just by working on the go.

I'm always trying to look for things to do, so it doesn't take much to motivate me. Since I sold the stores I've been staying busy. I never like to be still. What I'm attempting to do now is to teach my sons, my son-in-law and my daughter what they need to do to become successful. They're blessed that they don't have to work, but they need to work to keep their businesses going. They've already found some opportunities that will be easy to do. It's important to me that I pass along all that I can, especially to my grandson. That keeps you motivated.

I never really saw any obstacle as too big; I see an opportunity and I just push forward. Most of the time, if there's a problem that could lead to a negative you just have to work until it turns positive. If you apply yourself and think about it, you come up with different ways to get through it. You get excited because you see new opportunities.

Whatever the problem is, if I can't work it out mentally or quickly, I just use a scratch pad and write down pros and cons. Then I'll eliminate all the things I think would be tougher to do. It works pretty well. I'd do that when buying a store, after talking to the previous owner. I'd overestimate the cost of the building by ten percent and underestimate the possible income by ten or fifteen percent so I'd have a twenty-five percent cushion if I got any of the numbers wrong. Wal-Mart was located next to our first million dollar store; it paid for itself within two years. It cost a total of $1.3 million. We had a payment plan with the bank of $13,000 a month for ten years, but we actually paid it off within two years.

Defeat always teaches you patience, and there were *many*. The positive mental attitude keeps you on the right track. If you have a positive attitude you can get through anything. You always learn from other people. For example, if someone had what I thought was a great idea, I didn't hesitate to copy it and place my own twist on it. Just keep a positive attitude. I'm inspired by being successful and helping others. I've made quite a bit of money, but I don't have a real high lifestyle, so I don't spend a lot of money.

Health is very important. You can't accomplish anything without it. Eat right and exercise. I used to be active in baseball and I still play golf. We have a gym and we walk every day. I guess the hardest part is eating right and staying healthy without taking a lot of pills to aid in your health.

You have to prioritize. Don't waste time that you can delegate to someone else. That's important when you have 700 employees. It was hard to teach supervisors and managers how to delegate, and some even thought that no one could do it right but them. They might have been able to do it right, but it slows down the entire process. You can't accomplish much if you do everything yourself.

I definitely think being from central Appalachia has contributed to who I am and my work ethic. It gave me faith, and it gave me family. It's the best place in the world to live. I think that some of the smartest and most successful people came from the mountains. Most are very proud. I may be a hillbilly but I ain't a dumb hillbilly, and I'm proud of it. There's probably a church every half mile, and that says a whole lot about the people and how they live.

Figure out what you want to do and what you'll enjoy doing. Plan out the things that would make you successful, and not necessarily in business. You can be a teacher, a banker, a preacher. You can make lots of money or you can make enough to make you happy. Stick with it, and write down goals. I think you should write them down and not share them with someone unless you know they think the way you do. *Think and Grow Rich* tells you to put them on a 3x5 card. It's real important that you do that. Most people don't know what they want to do. They are like tumbleweeds, seeing something they like everywhere and never settling on something they want to do. That's the biggest hindrance.

Don't be selfish. You can't be successful by wishing that everyone else was a failure. You have to enjoy helping someone else be successful and you'll become more successful. I didn't intend to do all the things I did; they just kind of happened. I just worked hard and was very fortunate. You really can't have anything unless you've got a good partner or good friends and family. I just stuck to my principles, worked hard, was always honest, and tried to be good to everyone.

That's the way it works.

Don't be selfish. You can't be successful by wishing that everyone else was a failure. You have to enjoy helping someone else be successful and you'll become more successful . . .
I just worked hard and was very fortunate.

CHAPTER 4

Success in Education

Being confident gives you the courage to face risk and act when the opportunity arises. No one on earth is going to force success upon you; you will find it only to the degree that you actively seek it out.

—NAPOLEON HILL

Located in the heart of Napoleon Hill's birthplace, The University of Virginia's College at Wise (formerly Clinch Valley College of the University of Virginia) was founded in 1954 on a piece of land formerly designated as a poor farm. In its humble beginnings, the college was designed to serve those in the most remote part of Virginia.* At the center of this story is the intersection between a man determined to see the college become a success and a woman determined to change education for the better.

---

* The inspiring history of the college is chronicled in the book *No Ordinary College: A History of the University of Virginia's College at Wise* by Brian Steel Wills (University of Virginia Press, 2004).

DR. JOSEPH SMIDDY
First Director and Chancellor of the University of Virginia's College at Wise

Dr. Joe Smiddy (more affectionately known as "Papa Joe") was the first Chancellor of a small college in the coalfields of Wise County, Virginia, known then as Clinch Valley College of the University of Virginia. In 1960, he admitted the first African-American student, Miriam Morris Fuller, at a time when desegregation remained a controversial policy in Virginia. The longest-serving Chancellor of what would later be renamed The University of Virginia's College at Wise, Dr. Smiddy navigated the college through its first (sometimes tumultuous) fifty years of growth, while gaining immense popularity as a leader throughout the state of Virginia. He has worn many hats in his lifetime: World War II soldier, biology teacher, businessman, college dean, college director, deacon, and college chancellor. He is also well-known throughout the region as a bluegrass musician.

In Joe Smiddy's words . . .

Socially, I was very liberal, but with economics and finance I was conservative (I suppose because of the Depression.) I'm a Depression-oriented person. I always believed you had to save money because you may wake up one morning and it would all be gone. I learned to save as a young person. I learned that to be successful in business you had to know your product and know your customer. That's true in education, too. The product was learning and my consumer was the student. I have had a business philosophy all my life.

My father was the real hero of our family. When he was born in 1877, coal mining was just starting in eastern Kentucky, east Tennessee and southwest Virginia. My father came from a sharecropping family and he had very little schooling. The only schooling he had was from the missionaries who came through the mountains of east Tennessee, eastern Kentucky and southwest Virginia to teach the poor children who didn't have an opportunity to go to school. My father was a learner; a bright young fellow who wanted to go to school. When he was thirteen he went in the coal mines pushing the cars out for a quarter a day. He'd walk out of the mines with his dirty clothes and all and go to school. The kids laughed at him and said he was wasting his time.

As he worked in the mines, he kept studying and he bought books. He kept getting better jobs and crawling up the ladder. Around 1914, two friends came to him and said they were going to open a mine and wanted him to join in this new mine adventure. So my dad joined up with the two men, one of whom was a former member and president of the Mine Worker's union. My dad and his two partners sold stock in the company and opened the coal mine. They were very successful. They founded Jellico Coal and Coke Company and they had three mines.

I was nine years old in 1929 when my dad came home and said that there was coal on the ground and nowhere to ship it. My dad was lucky in that he had bought a home, some farm land, and a small store in the town of Jellico. He had it all paid for; he didn't owe anything. So we all went to the store and started to work. We carried groceries and we carried the milk and put it on people's porches at ten cents a quart. Nobody had any money, so it was all bartered. We'd go to the doctor and he'd put it on the book and the doctor would come to the store and buy groceries and we'd take milk to his house to pay for our doctor bill. We did that for everything. We went through the Depression most of the time without having any money, but we had a wonderful household.

When the Depression set in and my dad lost his coal business, my mother announced that she was going back to nursing. She made some nursing uniforms and that's exactly what she did. We didn't have a hospital then. Nurses mostly went to the homes and nursed people who were sick. My dad came in one day and told my mother that someone was stealing canned food out of the cellar. My mother said, 'Yes I know.' He said, 'I'm going to put a stop to that.' She said 'No, you're not going to put a stop to that. There are children going to bed hungry and we are going to help feed them. We're going to pray for times to get better so they won't have to steal.' She was a powerful woman and that's the kind of person she was.

When I was a senior in high school, my high school principal, who had a master's degree from Columbia University, said, 'Joe, where you going to college?' I said, 'Oh, I'm not going to college. I don't have any money to go to college.' He said, 'Next Saturday, I'll come up to your house at eight o'clock and we'll go visit the college.'

He picked me up and drove me to Lincoln Memorial University. He introduced me to the dean. Mr. Garrett said to the dean, 'This boy ought to go to college.' The dean looked up at me and said 'You want to go to college?' I had no transcripts, no money, and I was not the greatest student in the world. I said, 'Yes sir, I'd like to try.' He asked if I would work on the farm for twenty cents an hour to pay for tuition. I said yes. He said, 'Son, when you get out of high school, put your overalls in a paper bag and hitchhike on over here and we'll put you to work.' That was my admissions process.

My older sister lived in Chicago where I worked two summers in greenhouses growing roses and gardenias. It was wonderful, because I had that experience of going to the museums. I spent all my money going to see big bands like Louis Armstrong because that's really what I wanted to do. When I first went to college, I wanted to play in a jazz band.

At LMU, if you worked all day you made a dollar and sixty cents. So they took sixty cents for your board every day you worked, which left a dollar toward your tuition. The tuition, room and board and fees were $315 a year. I worked on the farm, I drove a team of horses, and I cut grass. I chucked rocks and ground them up with a tractor and put rocks in the potholes on the campus roads. At LMU, I don't think they bought anything but coffee and salt and sugar. Everything else was grown on the farm. They had a cannery, a slaughterhouse, a dairy and a laundry. Students did all the work.

I was playing in a jazz band at the college. And I did more playing than studying that first year. I met a wonderful girl by the name of Rosebud Stickley. She encouraged me to do a little studying.

The war clouds were gathering. Back then they developed the one year draft for men. I turned 21 that second year at LMU, and I signed up for the draft knowing I was going to be drafted and go to war. Rosebud and I wanted to get married.

We were both in the two year teaching program. Most people took the two-year teaching program, and then dropped out to teach and save up enough money to come back to college. We were broke, so we felt lucky if we could get the two years of college. We both got our teaching certificates. I got a job at a company store, which was a pretty good job back in those days. Six months later, I was in the army.

I was lucky during the war and didn't realize how much difference two years of college would make. Not many men in the army had been to college. I was assigned to be the assistant band director at Camp Lee, which was wonderful. But if I had to be separated from my wife, I figured I might as well go to war.

I went to my commanding officer and requested that I go. He asked why. I said, 'I'm from the mountains, and if I go back home and tell them I played in a band all through the war, they're going to run me out of town.'

I spent four Christmases in the service and got back home just before Christmas in 1945. I went back to LMU in March. I decided to teach biology because my biology teacher had been another of my heroes. I graduated and got a job teaching biology at Jonesville High School in the fall of 1947. Just to let you know the kinds of students who were at Jonesville, consider this: a group of nine students came to me and asked if I would teach physics. I told them I wasn't qualified. They said, 'Teach it anyway and we'll help you teach the course.' All but one (who was killed in a car accident) ended up with doctorate degrees.

I was promoted to principal, which I didn't like because I had no help. I had a secretary for one hour a day. Two friends of mine came and told me they had an oil company in Big Stone Gap, Virginia. 'If you'll come and manage that oil company,' they said, 'we'll sell you one third of it. We'll loan you the money to buy it, and we'll pay you twice what you're getting paid now.'

I had been going to graduate school. I went first to the College of William and Mary and did a summer of marine biology. Then I went three summers to Peabody-Vanderbilt and got my master's degree in biology. Then I started the PhD program at the University of Tennessee. I was working on my PhD when I left the school and went into the oil business. We moved to Big Stone Gap in the mid-1950's. I had two wonderful partners, and we were doing well in the business. I enjoyed making enough money to send my kids to school.

Clinch Valley College was a two-year school, and the chief administrator was the director of the college at that time. The Director, Samuel Crockett, came down to my office; I knew him because we were setting up extension courses through UVA for teachers. He said, 'Now, Joe, I know you've been working on your doctorate degree. We're starting a college up at Wise. We want you to come and teach classes.'

I went up when the college opened on September 13, 1954. What a day! I remember funeral home chairs set out behind Crockett Hall, and 109 students were there. About seventy of them were Korean War veterans and they were there, wanting to learn. What a wonderful opportunity! I loved to teach.

At the end of the second year, Dean Olen Campbell— who was the first dean of the college (who had a doctorate degree in Education from Duke)—found out that the university was not going to make a person with an education degree a permanent dean of the college. The liberal arts influence was too great. So they asked me to be dean. I said, 'I don't want to be a dean. I don't want to be an administrator.' I suggested they gave it to someone else, and they said, 'We've already offered and he won't take it. He's going to the Library of Congress.' So I said yes.

I taught every semester the 33 years I was there except for the last semester before I retired. I didn't get paid extra; I taught because I wanted to be a teacher. I didn't want to hire anybody at the college who didn't want to be a teacher. If you have to go around telling people you're the boss, you ought not to be there.

At the end of the third year, Mr. Crockett and Mr. Darden, the President of the University of Virginia, said, 'Sam is going to work in Roanoke, and you are going to be the director of the college.' So I assumed the director's job in 1957. I was still in graduate school at UT! When we hired people, they'd send them to Knoxville and I'd interview them! For one year, I was both dean *and* director.

What a wonderful faculty! I enjoyed working with those people. I enjoyed helping people. I always felt like my job was to reach the unreachable. I'd go into the high schools to recruit students. I'd get up in front of the group and talk to them about the college, and I'd look that group over. I'd see those boys—black and white—in the back of the room. I'd go to the back of the room and take hold of those boys and say, 'We have a place for you. We have a *place* for you.' We got some of them.

We were a two-year college trying to be a four-year school. We had students transferring to Harvard and other schools all over the country. The community college system is wonderful, but we weren't a community college; we were so strong in the liberal arts. We just didn't know anything about community college courses. So Dick Richmond, a Lee County man who was a superintendent of schools at the time, led a charge of all the superintendents in the state to support changing Clinch Valley from a two-year to a four-year school. That's how we got to be a four-year college in 1967. Then they changed my title from director to chancellor. I stayed on as chancellor until June of 1985, when I retired.

The greatest influence came from my first wife, Rosebud.* She opened doors in this part of the world that that boy from Jellico never could have opened. Without her, I really wasn't much, to tell you the truth. My second wife, Reba, and I were married in 1985 and she has been a true blessing to me. We've enjoyed playing music together.

As you become educated, certainly education should be liberating. It should cause you to reach out. I remember an essay in my mother's Bible, titled, 'If I Were 21 Again, I Would.' It said:

1. I would make friends with older people, because from older people you gather wisdom.

2. I would embrace unpopular causes because embracing an unpopular cause will require you to study. It will make you a better student.

---

* Rosebud Stickley Smiddy passed away in 1984.

Overcoming Obstacles

In 1960, one of the business professors came to me and said, 'There is a colored woman that wants to go to school. What shall I tell her?'

I said, 'Tell her to come on.'

She said, 'I understand in Virginia it's against the law for a colored student to go to a white state school, or a white student to go to a colored state school.'

I said, 'I really don't know. Tell her to come on.'

When it came registration time, a student came into the office and said, 'There's a colored woman in the registration line. What do you want to do?'

I said, 'Well, I'm going out there to see what color her money is. If it's green, we're going to take her.'

I didn't know it, but she was already a teacher at the black high school with a teaching degree. She wanted to become a business teacher, so she wanted to take our courses to qualify. She did become certified. It just so happened she was from the most elite African-American family this area has ever had.

I was greatly blessed that this institution is a part of the University of Virginia. They brought that philosophy of Thomas Jefferson—the freedom of the mind—as a part of the school they opened. That's what makes the college great. I went through difficult times because of that in this area due to the coal industry. Any area that depends on one industry will have difficulty, especially during the [1960's and early 1970's] when the students were protesting for regulating surface mining. If we had been a state school with local board members, we could never have been what our college is today. The university stayed with us. One thing that bothers me is the intrusion of big business into education. If coal had dominated our institution we never could have been what we wanted to be. Some of them tried to fire me because I was allowing the students to protest.

Now there were some good coal operators—you always have to qualify—that were educated similarly to me but some were not. One [coal operator] came to me during the student [and faculty] protests and said, 'Joe, if you get those students [and professors] back in the classroom where they belong . . . I'll raise and give seven million dollars to the college.'

I said, 'Well, we sure would like to have seven million dollars, which would improve our school, but we cannot deliver.'

He said, 'What do you mean you can't deliver?'

I said, 'I can't tell the professors and students what to think or what to do. We're not that kind of place.'

He replied, 'I didn't think anyone was in charge!'

That's the second best recommendation I've ever gotten.

I don't believe a coal miner's son—a man who started out in a sharecropper's family and went into the coal mines when he was 13 who was a true mountain product—would have done well without an education. I have felt at times that people would say, 'He's a country hick.' I think education was the key, the way 'out' for me. Without that high school principal or the GI Bill, I would not have gone on to school.

- **Helen Lewis**—Dr. Helen Lewis, who was born in rural Georgia, spent twenty years at Clinch Valley College of the University of Virginia as a sociologist and librarian before moving on to continue her work both in Appalachia and internationally. Dr. Lewis' success as an educator, researcher, and activist can be measured in the number of seeds she has planted throughout Appalachia and beyond in the past sixty years, and the influence she has had on Appalachian Studies programs. Her work in social and environmental activism has been both controversial and acclaimed, but no one can deny the multitude of programs and groups she has led to educate people in both rural and urban communities about the social, economic, and environmental structures that influence their lives.

DR. MIRIAM MORRIS FULLER
Professor and Children's Author

Dr. Miriam Morris Fuller's brief interaction with Joe Smiddy in 1960 made history at Clinch Valley College when she became the first African-American woman to enroll. Though the Supreme Court had ruled against the "separate but equal" doctrine of segregated schools six years earlier, the wheels of progress toward integration were barely turning in Virginia. Fuller's determination to defy an "unwritten policy" and apply for admission to an all-white college, and Dr. Smiddy's readiness to admit her in spite of the retaliation it might cause, kept Dr. Fuller on a path to success that her parents set for her at an early age. Both she and her brother, Charles, would go on to achieve doctorates in their respective fields.

The Results of Personal Initiative and a Positive Mental Attitude

Dr. Fuller made history again when she became the first African-American faculty member at the University of Missouri. After one failed attempt at applying for the job, Fuller came across an article describing the school's attempts at increasing their numbers of black students and staff. She contacted the school's recruiter, landed an interview, and began a seventeen-year career there.

A Creative Vision

During her tenure at the University of Missouri, Dr. Fuller founded two Preschool Development Centers. Recognizing a need for service among the mentally challenged women in the area, Dr. Fuller wrote a grant that allowed her to develop on-site training to mentally challenged women who wanted to become preschool aids.

A crying child led Fuller to the creative work for which she may be most recognized. A little girl came into her library trying to find a book she could read, and left in tears when she could find none. So, Dr. Fuller researched a popular reading method called "the linguistic method," whereby students were taught to read using rhyming sounds. She wrote the first of what became a ten-volume kit published by the Charles E. Merrill Publishing Company which was adopted by Urbana, Illinois schools for grades one, two and three. Dr. Fuller also wrote the children's biography *Phyllis Wheatley, America's First Black Poetess*.

In Miriam Morris Fuller's words . . .

Success is the positive outcome of goals achieved through hard work and a caring attitude.

An example of positive outcome occurred many, many years after I began a career as a teacher-librarian. This was during the so-called 'separate but equal' era in American history. I was working at Bland High School. Only a basic curriculum was offered, except that the boys were taught vocational education by my husband, Dr. Foster. The girls had a dim future after graduating from high school. The Parent-Teacher Association, of which my mother was president, began a financial drive to purchase six typewriters.

There were those who said I would never be accepted at a white college, but I remained mentally positive and had the faith that it would happen—and it did.

Since it was a known fact that the Board of Education would not hire a typing teacher, a faculty meeting was called. The principal asked if there was a teacher who had taken typing in college. I was the only one who had taken typing; therefore, I became the typing teacher.

The first year I taught typing, I applied to Clinch Valley College so that I could take typing and shorthand in night classes. This happened at a time when African-Americans were not accepted in white colleges and universities. However, Dr. Joseph Smiddy and the teacher, Mrs. Emma McCraray, accepted me. I registered in 1960. There were those who said I would never be accepted at a white college, but I remained mentally positive and had the faith that it would happen—and it did. After meeting Dr. Smiddy and Mrs. McCraray, I knew that they cared and had the courage of their convictions. I considered attending [CVC] going the extra mile, not for myself but for the students. As a result, the Bland High School students achieved success.

As I became better educated, I felt more secure in my ability to teach the students (mostly female) to become clerk typists and secretaries. A representative of the federal government visited African-American high schools during the end of the school year to test seniors for clerk typists and secretarial jobs at the Pentagon and Department of Labor. Many of the students passed the tests and received jobs in Washington D.C.

In August, 2007, at the Central and Bland High Schools reunion, several of my past students who attended expressed their appreciation. One of them had retired from the Department of Labor. That's what I call success!

The main obstacle in my life is racial prejudice. Being African-American, I have always lived with racism. That means that my entire life—to this moment—I have been coping and adjusting, a lifetime experience.

My home environment provided me with coping and adjusting skills. My parents, Charles and Edith Morris, instilled the following: God first and then education. They were positive, encouraging parents, coupled with being terrific role models. They were churchgoers as well as participants and they were hard workers. Their lives were dedicated to God so they were daily caring about and for others. They taught me that through God, all things are possible.

My immediate environment, which also included one sibling, Charles Jr. ("Buddy"), and my extended family of grandmothers, aunts, uncles, and cousins also nourished and guided my growth and development. I grew up in a family that lived out the 'love one another' statement. My brother, two cousins and I were taught to get along. We were not perfect, but there were small victories in the striving. The long-term practice of trying to get along has served me well in life, and has strengthened my coping and adjusting skills as I continually face racism. It also gave me strong self-esteem.

Now, in my retirement, I serve the poor, homeless, and downtrodden. I'm active in church activities as an elder and lay minister, and continue to work with children as a mentor to two fifth grade girls. When I work with these girls, a desire that they will have a bright and successful future motivates me into action. Statistics have proven that children who are mentored are more successful than those who are not. That fact alone motivates me.

In years gone by, I was fortunate to see my 'ministry' positively affecting the lives of children as I worked as a teacher, librarian, and preschool director. Finally, I was able to teach university students courses involving services to children and how to successfully interact with and positively shape their lives. Having a positive attitude is foremost toward anything one strives to achieve. Sincerity is a must and being tactful is necessary when counseling the parents of children served.

A cheerful facial expression and emotional control should be ever-present when serving children and interacting with adults. If one models tolerance and a sense of justice, situations are less likely to get out of control and working through problems becomes easier. Also, kindness that depicts a fondness and deep humility along with a calm tone of voice can help delete any difficulties.

My faith in God has sustained me throughout my life. When difficulties arise, I seek God and the beatitudes as expressed by Jesus Christ guide me.

There are several awards that I count among my greatest achievements, but being a good mother is of utmost importance. I strive to be the best mother possible for our sons, Foster, Jr. ("Chip"), Gary, and Drew. When they were very young, I was inspired to purchase a house in which to open a preschool. There were objections. A board member questioned whether a community accustomed to babysitting would accept a preschool. This lack of confidence was a distraction. Refusing to think negatively, I responded, 'I don't begin something by thinking I cannot succeed.' This preschool lasted 22 years.

Reasoning through problems requires emphasis upon positives in a situation. One needs to be flexible when striving toward goals. When others are involved, all talents and skills should be recognized and utilized. Two or more heads can be better than one. The wise person realizes and works well with others toward goals to be achieved. This is done by having respect for the ideas of others.

Adversity and defeat can spur a positive-thinking person forward toward success. Upon arriving at a new community, I applied for a job that I did not get. Upon hearing that a possible reason was that I was too educated and had too much experience, I did not stop. They wanted a person right out of school so that the salary would be smaller. I learned a valuable lesson from that experience. Not giving up, I applied for a higher position where being 'over-educated and having too much experience' was an asset. I got the job.

I read a variety of books, magazines, and newspapers and I get involved in church and community activities. This inspires me to become deeply aware of the effects of homelessness, poverty, lack of health care and racism. Caring about the welfare of others is a top priority in my life, and caring and doing for helpless children is my highest aim.

Looking back over Hill's seventeen principles, I consider the following to be the most significant toward achieving success:

+ A positive mental attitude
+ Sincerity
+ Habit of smiling
+ Tolerance
+ Sense of humor
+ Faith, sense of justice
+ Effective speech
+ Emotional control
+ Versatility
+ Fondness for people
+ Humility

As I look back on my life, I realize that the negatives and positives are of almost equal importance. The positives, however, can cancel out the negatives if one has a focused determination to succeed. Finally, as an 'older' person with a cache of wisdom, I'd like to say: have a strong faith in God, keep your heart right, and don't jump to conclusions.

- **John Forbes Nash, Jr.**—Born in Bluefield, West Virginia, John Nash, Jr. won acclaim for his theoretical contributions to the field of mathematics. Nash graduated from Princeton and taught at MIT for several years. He was awarded the Nobel Prize in economics in 1994. His battle with mental illness has drawn attention to research and understanding of the disease. His life was immortalized in the award winning movie *A Beautiful Mind*, starring Russell Crowe.

CHAPTER 5

Success in Medicine

Don't try to cure a headache. It's better to cure the thing that caused it.   —NAPOLEON HILL

The disparities between the most distressed parts of Appalachia and the rest of the nation with regard to accessible, quality health care have been well-documented over the years. In recent years, the region has seen some success in attracting more primary-care physicians, but the doctor-patient ratio continues to be extremely disproportionate compared to the rest of the nation at approximately one primary-care physician for every 2,100 people in distressed counties and one specialist per 2,800 people.* Nevertheless, this specialist discusses how success can be achieved in spite of those staggering statistics, most notably by showing patients how the mind can be a powerful ally in the healing process.

---

* The Encyclopedia of Appalachia (2005), p. 1635.

ROBERT PATTON, M.D.,
Gastroenterologist

Dr. Robert Patton was born in Clinchco, Virginia where his father mined coal for a living. He was the first gastroenterologist* in Kingsport, Tennessee, where he now lives and where he followed in the footsteps of his great-great grandfather, who was the first physician to set up a practice in the city in 1820. Dr. Patton credits *Think and Grow Rich* in part for leading him to where he is today. Though he is retired, he is actively researching the mind/body connection and its role in healing.

In what ways have you gone the extra mile above or beyond what was expected in your journey toward success?

In my practice I try to get to know my patients, and I try to establish a relationship with them. No one heals another person; your body has to heal itself, and so a healer is someone who facilitates healing. You can do that in different ways. There are lots of healers other than physicians. A healer can be a minister, your mother, or a friend. The art of medicine is not only science. I did try to know my patients so they would understand that I cared for them. That took more time, but it was with the thought that this would result in success.

What motivates you?

When you get an idea, it creates desire which has a certain amount of energy. Then, you get an intention that you want to

---

* Gastroenterology is the study of disorders of the entire digestive system.

promote this desire. Then you get a will, which is willpower, and that is also motivating and leads to accomplishing what you're trying to do. When I start focusing energy on things that I want to accomplish, that's what motivates me. I use visualization to determine the outcome.

How do you maintain a positive mental attitude, or the "I Can" attitude, when facing challenging circumstances?

I think a key is turning your thinking from problem to solution. If we think about problems, negative emotions arise that make us feel bad. So, we ask ourselves two questions: what might make this situation better and what good will come out of it? By doing that, we change our minds from being problem-oriented to being solution-oriented. It changes our internal chemistry, and this is how we can feel good even dealing with difficult situations. It helps you maintain a positive attitude toward what you're trying to do. I use that technique in my practice in terms of stress management because I have to practice not being problematic.

What techniques do you use to focus without letting bad habits or distractions get in the way?

I learned a long time ago to write my goals down, so I keep a goal list, and I look at it frequently. It may change from time to time, but I think we need to have reminders. Research suggests that writing things down and being reminded of them tends to help you stay on track.

What is your method for reasoning through a decision or a problem?

It's important to define the problem. We tend to generalize. For instance, someone may say, 'What's your problem?' It's my work, but it's not the *work*; it's an individual at work or some expectation at work. It's very important to know exactly what it is that we're concerned about and then we can start working on solutions. You can't solve a mess.

How do you work with others to achieve your goal?

You look as best you can at the other person's perspective and try to figure out how accomplishing this goal is going to be good for both people, which leads to better teamwork.

When I went into practice, I was the first gastroenterologist in town and very busy. I needed help in managing the load and maintaining my sanity. At that time, probably, I was certainly not following these principles.

As the years went by, some issues came up that had to do with an HMO coming into town, so we physicians had to get organized to figure how we were going to react and interact with this changing environment. Another doctor and I worked together on that project, focusing more on our commonalities than our differences. We developed a common goal in terms of developing a successful practice, and so we mutually developed the practice that we had. That was a big lesson.

Where do you get your inspiration for cultivating new ideas?

I like to figure out what's going to happen in the future, and see how I can be a part of it. We know that the body is more powerful than any pharmacy. We know the body can cure cancer. The body is capable of doing lots of things and we'll find different avenues to the relationship between the mind and the body.

I read about nanotechnology,* which is going to change the way we live, so we'll be working with molecules and atoms. Everything will be smaller, stronger, better, and allow us to do things that seem like science fiction.

Is your health an important factor in your success, and what are your habits for maintaining such mental and physical health?

I study nutrition, supplements, the things that work and things that don't work. One of the things that we are learning now is the importance of keeping our muscle mass tuned up even into old age, so I'm a believer.

What's your best advice for budgeting time and money?

We need to budget our time based on our values. The way to budget money is to save first and plan for saving.

In what way do you use your cultural environment as a motivating factor to achieve success?

I'm glad I was born in Clinchco, Virginia. I'm glad that my father was a coal miner. I like the people, I like the area, and I don't consider the environment a hindrance. Another person might see that differently, but I think it was more positive than negative. When I look back on it, it gives me a good sense to

---

* The study of engineering matter at the molecular and anotomic scale.

know that I could do what I wanted to do, so it didn't hold me down.

When people visit me from Dickenson County, I enjoy being their doctor, and I feel that I do know the language and I do know the situation. I can see that there is poverty, unemployment and school systems that are not always optimum; however, though the environment can be a struggle for people, I'd like to see that incurred in ways that would be positive for people. I wouldn't trade it.

You had the choice to go anywhere, but you stayed in east Tennessee . . .
Maybe it's just my philosophy, but everything's the way it's supposed to be. Every right turn that I have taken in my life has led me to where I am right now, so this is where I'm supposed to be. I'm to be me.

Looking back over these seventeen principles, which would you point as the most significant in giving advice to those who want to follow your path?
My advice is to think accurately, because thought is the most powerful thing in the world. First of all, we can't really define it, so in my best definition it is some form of mental energy being applied. You take that energy and you put it with physical energy, which is action, and it leads to transformation, and so for most people that's magic because you're taking something from thin air, which is a thought and you're turning it back into something that's physical. For instance, I just thought, 'I'm thirsty,' so I'm taking a drink. That's a miracle because it's how you *think* that makes the difference.

Sometime in college, I just ran across *Think and Grow Rich*. I thought, 'That sounds good to me. I want to be rich.' That's what I was interested in. So when I read it the first time, I was impressed by all these successful people who were saying that there's something to learn about success.

That was my first encounter with the book, but along the way as I have changed, my philosophy has changed. I've been back to the book and I understand it. Hill does talk a lot about material wealth; on the other hand, you find that he also talks about balance in life. So the more I read the more I learned how to be successful in what you do. I think it goes beyond just rich; you can be wealthy in many ways, and so it helps you attain that.

[Napoleon] Hill does talk a lot about material wealth;
on the other hand, you find that he also talks about
balance in life ... It goes beyond just [being] rich;
you can be wealthy in many ways ...

On the Mind/Body Connection ...

I saw what was happening in alternative medicine. People will do just about everything and sometimes hurt themselves, because they're not getting what they need from the medical establishment. If you know the state that health care is in regarding financing and socialized medicine, you'll know that it's not going to become holistic. So there will be opportunities to help you get your act together and teach you how to live a healthy life. That's the thing that interests me the most.

- **Eula Hall,** a community health-care organizer who is best known as the founder and coordinator of the Mud Creek Clinic in Floyd County, Kentucky, was born in Pike County in 1927. Hall raised five children in extreme poverty and with little formal education after escaping an abusive relationship. She developed a sense of community leadership as a result of the help she received from friends and neighbors and inspiration during the War on Poverty of the 1960's. She worked with the service and advocacy group Appalachian Volunteers to establish programs and organizations to advocate for poor people, miners and victims of domestic abuse. In 1975 she received a presidential citation from the American Public Health Association and in 1999 she was given the Kentucky Commission on Women award. She has been listed among the most notable Americans by *People* and *Family Circle* magazines.

- **Andrew Taylor Still,** the founder of Osteopathic medicine, was born on August 6, 1828, in a log cabin in Lee County, Virginia. As a frontier doctor in the mid1800's, Still had a typical frontier medical practice, sometimes traveling great distances to reach the bedsides of his patients where he used methods recommended in medical books. Later, he was a surgeon for the Union Army during the Civil War. After losing much of his family to various illnesses and after seeing the brutal medical techniques used in the Civil War, Still rejected most of what he had learned about medicine and began to search for new and better methods, particularly with regard to nutrition and preventative medicine. Still's explorations were grounded in the study of anatomy and the body's tendency toward selfhealing. The key was to find and correct anatomical deviations that interfered with the free flow of blood and "nerve force" in the body. From the beginning, Still met with considerable opposition to his new theories and techniques and he separated from the field of traditional medicine. In 1874, Still moved to Missouri, where he hoped his ideas would be better received. Advertising himself as a magnetic healer and a "lightning bonesetter," Still slowly built up his reputation. Word spread about the doctor whose system of drugless, manipulative medicine—officially named "osteopathy" in 1885—was able to cure many apparently hopeless cases. Finding he had more patients than he could handle, Still trained his children and a few others to assist him in his practice. Finally, there were enough people who wanted to learn his methods that he was persuaded to start a school. The American School of Osteopathy (ASO) (now the Kirksville College of Osteopathic Medicine) was founded in Kirksville, Missouri in 1892 in a two-room frame building. The first class of five women and 16 men—including three of Still's children and one of his brothers—graduated in 1894. Now, five osteopathic medical schools exist in the Appalachian region. Still remained active in the ASO almost until his death at the age of 89. The Andrew Taylor Still Memorial Park in Jonesville commemorates the county's native son.

CHAPTER 6

Living a
Grandfather's Legacy

Successful people create their own opportunities by focusing on goals with an intensity that borders on obsession. In this way, every action moves them toward their goal. —NAPOLEON HILL

DR. JAMES B. HILL

Dr. James "J.B." Hill's story is inspiring but not because he is the grandson of Napoleon Hill, which would seem to have put him on a trajectory toward certain success. He was inspired (like others in this book) to follow his grandfather's advice in his early twenties by way of the book *Think and Grow Rich*. His narrative reveals a life journey that winds its way through several setbacks followed by a series of calculated decisions and extreme sacrifices as he keeps his eye on a commitment to achieve. Along the way, Hill chooses to take as much time as he needs to achieve each goal instead of following the "age-appropriate" timelines. As a result, Hill finds that he actually achieves every childhood dream he imagined.

In J. B. Hill's words . . .

I met [Napoleon Hill] in 1961, and he was very cordial. He seemed like an old man to me at the time. He was 78 then, with a library full of books. He gave me a ten dollar bill (which was a treasure to me in that day) and he told me that a ten dollar bill represented a man's labor for one day, and that I should value it. My mother told me to not spend it because it would be the only gift I'd get from him, but that wasn't true. I got a much bigger gift.

I grew up hearing about Napoleon Hill so I would look for information about him in encyclopedias and printings. In the bookstores I'd see his names on the books. I actually read *Think and Grow Rich* at the age of twelve, and it was a nice story, but it didn't affect me significantly at that age.

Then, I was sent off to school. My parents were worried about money; they had three children who were going to be in college at the same time. I ended up going to the Merchant Marine Academy in Kings Point, New York on a full scholarship. The last two years there I spent on cargo ships all over the world. I became self-sufficient very quickly.

Paris Island is where I ended up in 1969. Basically, I flunked out of school. It happened because I was having too much fun overseas in Vietnam, the Philippines, and South America doing the Joseph Conrad* thing. In 1971, I was about twenty-three years old and one year from getting out of the Marine

---

* Joseph Conrad (1857–1924) was an adventurous English novelist whose voyages inspired his stories and novels.

Corps. I started thinking about what I was going to do: get out of the Marine Corps, or stay in the Marine Corps. I really didn't know.

For years, I carried around a paperback copy of *Think and Grow Rich* signed by Napoleon Hill. When I read the book a second time, all of a sudden it had meaning to me. I don't know if it was a connection to Napoleon Hill that made me pay attention to the book a second time. But the night I finished reading that book, I decided I was going to change my life and take hold of it. I had no goal, and I didn't know what I wanted to do in life. You need a goal; it doesn't matter what it is, but you re-define that goal as you get closer to it. I thought, 'I need to do what the book tells me to do. Just pick a goal. Write down the steps to achieve that goal, and then do them one by one.' So that's what I did. I made a commitment at the age of twenty-three to dedicate myself to achieving that goal. I didn't know what that was at the time, but I was willing to do it.

For years, I carried around a paperback copy of
Think and Grow Rich signed by Napoleon Hill . . .
[T]he night I finished reading that book, I decided I was going
to change my life and take hold of it . . . I thought, 'I need to do
what the book tells me to do. Just pick a goal. Write down the
steps to achieve that goal, and then do them one by one.'

I said, 'What do I want to do in life?' I had no great religious affiliation at that time. I had no great moral cause at that time. I lived the life of a young man who was able to sail around the world and do things that some people will never do. I said, 'I don't know,' so I sat down and wrote the goals of everything that I would want to do.

I wanted to become a doctor when I was a child. I also wanted to become a space man—bear in mind, this was *after* man landed on the moon. I read every science-fiction book I could get my hands on. I listed about six or seven things I wanted to do, and I looked at each one of those things to see if it was attainable and something I could achieve, or ridiculous. Nothing was as ridiculous as a space man, but the reason I bring it up is that is comes to play later on. Remember that.

I knew that if I didn't complete my education, I'd feel that there was something left undone. I came from an Irish background and an educated family, and I realized that I was just an uneducated marine, and unless I got an education I would feel inferior to everyone in my family. My friends had gone on to Cornell, Duke, WVU, and MIT, so that's what I wanted. Then I asked myself, 'What are my options, what is the best way to get an education?' I could stay in the Marine Corps and go to night school; stay in the Marine Corps and enter a program; get out of the Marines, get my GI Bill, and work; get out, get the GI, work, and go back to mom and dad. So I thought about those options, and I chose the program funded by the Marine Corps.

The next step was to identify the pre-requisites. I needed a recommendation from a commanding officer. I didn't have any problem with that because I was successful and because I outworked everyone. I take pride in the work I do, and I like to be recognized for my work. My high school SAT scores were 500 and 550 (math and verbal) which was average for that day, but not good enough for the program, so my plan became how to raise my scores. I took some sample tests, and found out that eighty percent of the math tests were verbally related, so I decided that I needed to work on math and on verbal. I planned to dedicate a year of my life to achieving it.

I had one year to achieve this goal and be selected with this program before I would be too old. For a year, I didn't date, I didn't drink, and I didn't smoke. I took a correspondence course in chemistry, I went to night school, and I took calculus. I did that for thirty days, and for those thirty days I didn't watch television. I just sat and did math problem, after math problem, after math problem. I got a book called *1000 Commonly Used Words on the SATs*. I took ten days leave, divided the words into 100 per day and memorized the 100 words per day. I quickly became aware that the words were part of a working vocabulary of the literate world, but you don't hear them if you don't know what they mean; you pick up what they mean from context or the juxtaposition of the words. Over the next six months or so of reading, hearing, and seeing those words, I finally got a connection. When I retook the SATs at the end of that year my verbal had gone to 680 and my math to 650, which—in those days—was good enough to get me into Vanderbilt. By the end of the year I had taken the SATs, applied for the program, and was enlisted in the Navy Scientific Education Program. Upon acceptance into it I went to a Naval Academy Prep School in Maryland, where I competed for slots to the nineteen schools with ROTC units. I chose Vanderbilt, which was close to home. I sent my application, and I was accepted.

I had accomplished my goal: I got into a program that was funded. When I got to Vanderbilt, I asked myself: 'What is my goal here?' I wanted to do the best job I could, and I wanted to complete the program. So I said, 'Since I'm being paid to go to school, I'm going to commit myself, and do nothing but school work. I'm not going to sit around, go to the student union, watch television, or play football.' Vanderbilt's a very difficult school, and a very good school.

An engineering major, I quickly found that I was outworking everyone around me. Every student was probably studying two to three hours a week and I was studying five hours a day. I didn't have enough work to do on a daily basis to fill my eight hours. So, I'd fill the hours by reading assignments in advance. I went to every class, I took notes, and I rewrote my notes after class, so by the time finals would come I'd seen it all hundreds of times. I was then a straight A student at Vanderbilt in engineering because I'd learned from preparing the previous year for this program the same way.

I read *Think and Grow Rich* and I decided that I was going to do what it told me to do. And this time I knew that I could do what I didn't do the first time I was in school. The last semester I was at Vanderbilt the Marine Corps put out an AA form (a request for training after commission.) I wanted to be a pilot but I was too old, so I decided to be a 'back-seater,' a radar navigator in the back of an F4 Phantom. I graduated from Vanderbilt in December of 1976, and I immediately went to the basic school in Quantico, Virginia, a kind of finishing school for Marine Corps officers.

My flight physical exam qualified me for the six-month program, but they didn't need any back-seaters so they gave me an option. Since they couldn't honor the contract, I could leave active duty or they would give me any qualification that I needed. I wanted to be a pilot, but I was three years too old, so I had to take another flight physical. I passed and was selected to learn how to fly. My package with the flight physical sat on the desk at the Headquarters at the Marine Corps.

At about the same time, the services had allocated two slots for mission specialists in the space program, and each of the services was allowed to pick two people for training to be a specialist on the space shuttle program. The Marines have a lot of fine leaders, but not engineering types, and they wanted people with strong technical backgrounds, particularly at the graduate level. I didn't have graduate level work, but I had strong credentials. They screened records of those who physically qualified for flight, and I was asked if my file could be sent for consideration for the space shuttle program. At that point, I realized that I had a boyhood goal of being a space man—a childhood fantasy before man even walked on the moon. I had qualified myself for consideration for the one thing in life I wanted to do.

I firmly believed in Napoleon Hill's philosophy of success: that anyone can do anything by picking a goal, applying themselves and going after it. I couldn't understand anyone who couldn't or wouldn't do that. I realize that people have limitations, but it doesn't stop them from achieving great success (depending on how you define success) and we can all do more than we do if we apply ourselves. However, at this time I was rather arrogant.

Flight school was tough; I was in the flight program about a year on the ground before I started flying. A book about the astronauts was made into a movie called *The Right Stuff*. The astronauts had 'the right stuff,' meaning doing things that other people can't do. A pilot will move like Michael Jordan: he just knows what to do when he's in the air and can still think of everything going on around him. They have psycho-motor coordination between their bodies and minds. One of the reasons for the age restrictions on flight school is because it's difficult to train an old dog that doesn't have that. Flight school was difficult for me, not because of the academics, but because I wasn't able to execute procedures while I was flying the plane. The plane they put me in was a T-28 Trainer which had been designed as a WWII fighter. It had a twelve-cylinder engine and so much torque that it'll go sideways if you give it too much thrust as you're going down the runway. You've got to give so much thrust while paying attention to the planes on the ground and in the air. You have to pay attention to three different radios and differentiate among particular voices. You must know how to switch back and forth, all going 150 miles per hour with no GPS, and before you know it, you're lost. It was excruciatingly difficult.

I tried everything I could to develop my psychomotor coordination. I'd take a basketball and go running and dribble the ball, first with my right hand, then with my left. I'd do the same with golf balls and tennis balls; I'd run up and down the street bouncing the balls and try to catch them before they could bounce away. At the same time, I'd go over my proce-dures, like what I would do if the engine stalls, because the next day they could take you up to 10,000 feet and cut the engine. So you better know your procedures, and if you don't, then you're in trouble.

I was still cocky. One day I pretended I was a Navy fighter, and I was making a roll particularly tight. When I came down,

I hit hard and bounced, which was considered a crash. But because I was a trainee and there were no injuries involved, there was only a board of inquiry. I took some heat from that, and I asked myself if I wanted to be a mediocre pilot. I had talent and I could do this, but did I want to be mediocre? Would I be happy being a pilot? I didn't think I would. I didn't know if the decision was self-serving, or if I wanted out of the program because it was so difficult. I put in a drop request, and they tried to change my mind by saying, 'You can do this. You've got the ability to do this, and you were heading to the jets.' In my mind, I was never going to be happy being a pilot.

So I bounced into the artillery. I knew my limitation, so I wasn't quite as arrogant. I found I had developed leadership skills in managerial school so I learned to extract from people what they were willing and capable of giving, and I learned quickly that you motivate people, give them their work tools, and then you supervise. Think about Napoleon Hill's philosophy: you begin planning, you arrange how to execute the plan, you make a plan, and you issue the orders in which you commit yourself. So, at that point, I was committed to executing my plan. It's the same thing: if you want to be a good troop leader, you have to make sure your system works, and you do it.

I had a desire to teach at the Naval Academy, so I used the Napoleon Hill philosophy again. I simply put in an AA form to go to graduate school; I did research to see who got accepted there, and what the requirements were to get in; and then planned my future around my admission to graduate school. I also chose the most difficult major to increase my chances of getting into the Naval Academy, thinking that others would choose the most common major. I chose Operations Research, which is applied mathematics. My goal wasn't to get a master's degree in math; it was to teach at the Naval Academy, but to do that I had to get a master's in math. I was selected into the program, so I went to Monterey, California, spent two and a half years in grad school studying math (which I wasn't particularly interested in, but it was useful.) I went to the Naval Academy and spent four years there.

At this time, using the Napoleon Hill philosophy had become second nature to me. I've used it to shape things in my life. Before *Think and Grow Rich*, I was going nowhere, and I had no goals. I was not a nice man. I had rough edges.

At the Naval Academy my future started raising its head. I was approaching the twenty-year mark and my retirement was looming. I started evaluating. I was a top officer who had been chosen for every program I applied to, and one time I was so in demand as a lieutenant that I was made a battalion personnel officer. They gave me command of headquarters and service companies, so I had three offices that I worked through and three full time jobs. I still had the habit of working harder than other people, and in return I'd received the confidence of others. Did I want to stay in the Marine Corps or did I want to get out?

Defining Success

I'd done some research at the Naval Academy on success, which I defined as 'the ability to survive your first year.' What kind of individual survives the rigor of the Naval Academy for the first year? The only thing available to me was an inventory that asks pages and pages of questions that define your personality, and things that you'd rather do in your time. I added other things to it, like SAT scores, which were not good indicators of success. The single best predictor at the Naval Academy was individual class standing and the amount of extra activities they were enrolled in. You can't study 24 hours a day, so you have to learn to pick and choose what's important to study, and then juggle your time for your academic and professional leadership. They put you under so much pressure and then judge how you react under pressure to determine if you will make a good officer. Enlisted people do not need to think under pressure, just act on orders. If they survive then those people will make great officers. In boot camp you do things that you normally wouldn't do and you learn to trust those people who ask you to do that. The year I was there, a student from California had graduated number one in a class of 5,000. She had one extra-curricular activity: she played flute in the band. She flunked out of the Naval Academy.

I got a call asking if I still wanted to retire or if I wanted to be promoted. I became a major, and instead of forcing another tour overseas I was able to go through the AFMC and then I became General Wilhelm's aid because they needed someone with an ornate sense of detail who would focus. One reason why I didn't do well in flight school was because my strength is my ability to focus on something and solve it to the point where I don't see anything other than what I'm working on.

Another Childhood Dream Realized

A battalion sergeant asked me what I wanted to do when I went into the Marine Corps, and I mentioned becoming a doctor. I said that I was too old, but he said that I could still become a doctor because there was a woman in his residency program in her forties and that if I wanted to go for it that I should. I thanked him, and then I went home and thought long and hard about it.

I wrote five well-worded letters to institutions identifying who I was and that I was getting ready to make the decision of whether to stay in the marine corps. I said that I was leaning to getting out and pursuing one of my first goals to become a doctor, and I wanted a frank assessment (I included my achievements in school) if it was reasonable that a man my age could come back and start medical school. I got responses from four universities, including a letter from West Virginia University. John Tolbert—who was the head of the family practice and started the residency program there—said, 'Go for it.' I talked to my wife and she simply said, 'Wherest thou go, I go.' I think she had an understanding of what it would mean, but that started my planning for this goal.

My family was against my going to medical school, not because they didn't believe in me, but because it takes many years to get through the program. I didn't have that many years, and it could be a waste of taxpayer money. All these things they said may have been true, but I did have a backup plan. They kept giving reasons that I'd come back, like it's not lucrative the way it used to be, you've got to work so many hours, and the reimbursements aren't what they used to be, but they didn't understand why I wanted to be a doctor.

I'm a trained decision-maker. They didn't understand that I wanted to help people, just as I had changed lives of my enlisted men. For example, there was a cook in my unit who was a heavy drinker, and they were having troubles with him in the mess hall. I made him a special project to help himself work better and become a better person, and in the end I was able to do it. Later on after I recognized him for being a good worker, he came to me in tears because that was the first time he'd ever been recognized for anything. A year later he was a lance corporal, and I had the pleasure of swearing him into the Marine Corps.

When I teach people about focus and goal setting, I mention *Think and Grow Rich*. I tell them that the author interviewed successful people to see how they became successful and learned that they all became successful the same way: they wrote down the steps and they went for their goals.

The idea of going to medical school became my goal. I wanted to move back to West Virginia and become a family doctor in a little community where I know everyone, and be able to affect people in their everyday lives. I still had my pension, and my GI Bill. Nancy got a job in a real estate office, and we lived in a two bedroom townhouse. Then I started taking courses. My backup plan was to transfer credits in and get my engineering degree in chemistry. I looked at all the courses I needed for med school, and knew that in those three years, that I'd be able to get that engineering degree in chemistry if I couldn't get into medical school. I had math going for me because science is nothing but a form of applied math, and teaching math gave me an advantage, too. I was about 47 years old then.

This process actually became tough. I was in class with eighteen of the absolute brightest students that WVU had, none older than eighteen. I was taking honors courses with two labs each week, and each lab took five hours to write up. I needed organic and bio-chemistry classes, and I needed the other half of a chemistry class I started thirty years before. It took a year to do all that because I needed the background.

I gained a mentor from the community who happened to be my mother's doctor, Dr. John Traubert, who was well-known by my family at the time. My wife was supportive and he was encouraging, so I applied myself to my academics. I took chemistry for chemistry majors, biology for biology majors, computer science for computer science majors. I took core courses that were hard, knowing that I needed A's to prepare myself. So for the second year I went back to Dr. Traubert, who said that I needed to stop taking classes to help me now, but to take classes to help me when I got into medical school. I stopped computer science, but I took bio-chemistry and genetics, knowing I needed those. That summer I took organic chemistry. I studied for the MCAT to take as practice that year, and then for real the next which was part of my three year plan. I took my MCAT, and I didn't do so well. I knew I wasn't going to do very well, since I was only taking it for practice. My life science skills weren't great. I hadn't had enough courses.

At that time I had heard before the test that Lewisburg would take people, and I applied knowing that I'd need this for practice, and I got an interview to the school two years ahead of my plan. I decided I'd go for the interview because it would be good practice, and to sell myself as much as I could. There was a vicious board that day, and after a general interview they asked if I had any questions; I said that I wanted to ask about my age and my MCAT scores. They said that my age had nothing to do with it. They didn't discriminate on age and a lot of their students are not of the traditional med school age. They also said that MCAT scores don't necessarily tell how good a doctor you can be. I said that I still wanted to talk about that, so I continued to talk, saying that in addition to my MCAT scores I had over 300 college credits with most in graduate classes, most in science, and most A's. I said I had the ability to do the work, and that my scores are only temporary because they'd go up when I went back to study more. I'd worked for sixteen to eighteen hours a day for most of my career, and that I had the goal to do it, and that if they'd accept me, I'd graduate.

A Plan for Survival

I went back to school that fall and took bio-chemistry, and out of the blue that November I got a letter saying that I was accepted to the medical school. So, my plan to go to medical school had happened, but it now became a plan to survive. I needed to focus on what I was doing that first year—mainly because most students had more experience in medicine—and I knew I could focus if I didn't have a distraction. My wife stayed in Morgantown and I went to Lewisburg. I was the oldest in my class, but I had an amazing work ethic. The younger you were, the easier it was; I'd been used to being among the top five in my classes, but now I was the top of the bottom three.

When I was a marine, I switched from fact-based knowledge to experience-based knowledge. The high-ranking people know the details, and you know only what they divulge, so your whole thinking process switches over. Now, I was the man who needed to know how many cc's to give Patient X so he doesn't die. For me, medicine was memorizing a tree without having any leaves. There was no real rhyme for me until I started studying more and making connections. I had to go through and learn from scratch what others have known since before they entered medical school, so what was assumed that every student knew, I needed to learn it. I had to compensate by working. I'd study non-stop from the time I got up to the time I went to bed. There was no TV for one year. At Lewisburg, they are very aware of how students do there. In 'block week' you do nothing but study, the faculty comes in and cooks for you, and then you go back to studying. It was my second year that I almost cracked and I came close to quitting. However, I finished my second year, I did my rotations, and I finally graduated.

Going the Extra Mile

After medical school you're basically a trained doctor, but you're not a specialist. Since everything's a specialty, you've got to go through residency, but you must apply and compete with others. I really wanted to go do my residency back home with my wife in Clarksburg. They had a good program there, and at the end of my two years, I exposed myself to the residency program there through my rotations, but I still had to compete with the others from my class. Actually, my class had the most competitive group because there were more people applying for this internship than there were slots available. I was going to have to stand out from everyone else, and do everything I could do to get the heads to notice me; I wasn't the smartest in the group, and my age was a factor in my mind, as well.

This residency program was incredibly important to me, and I definitely had some handicaps, but I had something working for me: I could outwork anybody around and that's what I decided to do. I'd keep my mouth shut—there's nothing more embarrassing than sitting in class, especially when you're tired, and answering a question and showing just how much you *don't* know. I'll give you an example. There was a doctor who was brilliant, but he was hated. I wanted to learn, so I wanted to work with him. I quickly saw how tired the residents were and I knew that I needed to come in at 8 a.m. and start seeing patients so when the residents got over there at one or two in the afternoon, the patients would be checked out, and orders would be written out. I couldn't sign them, but the residents could, and then I would brief the doctor. That plan paid off because two residents who noticed my work went to the medical board and said that they needed me. I knew that I had to show that I could handle the stress of residency.

In my last year of medical school, I was rotating with family medicine. A doctor we were working with typically tried to go home for the weekend on Friday afternoons. One Friday three people came in and needed to be worked up, and the attending told him to go home, and for me to work up the patients. I said, 'Okay,' because I knew that I need to be the stability to hold people together. I got selected for the program and I was excited.

Developing a Pleasing Personality

You can't control your background, but you can control how hard you work and what you do. I believe there are only five important personality traits. Being tactful is courteous, smiling is courteous, and listening is courteous. Courtesy is one of the key traits to a pleasing personality. You cannot believe that the most courteous person in my residence program was always me, and part of that was training I got in the Marine Corps, but I had to develop that. Look people in the eyes, listen to them when they have something to say, make appropriate comments, and then follow up.

Looking Back on a Definition of Success . . .

You have to define success before you can measure it. From my perspective, achieving happiness is success. Happiness defines success, but success doesn't define happiness. I know many people who are successful bankers, successful lawyers or businessmen who aren't happy. In the end, if they aren't happy, then they aren't successful because why do we live?

I didn't know anything about life until I had children. I thought I knew, but I didn't know until I adopted David. I'm happy with my wife, and I'm happy with my children. Am I successful? Is my dad successful? He's 89, and has three kids. He never had two dimes to rub together but married a most wonderful woman. They had a wonderful love affair. Dad flew 55 fighter planes, and mom was a war widow with a little girl. Dad would fly from London, stand up for twelve hours to see her at the station for fifteen minutes, and then repeat the trip back to London. They were forbidden to date, so they'd write back and forth in secret.

What's your advice to those who want to achieve success?

If you don't try then you're not going to do it. If you don't try to become an astronaut then you never will be; otherwise, you don't know your limits and capabilities.

If you don't try to become an astronaut then you never will be;
otherwise, you don't know your limits and capabilities.

I have a success story to tell you about a woman who works in the hospital who sells Mary Kay cosmetics. She earned a car after only six months of selling Mary Kay. One night when she came in to work on some paperwork a steps to do it, and you've been doing it every single day.' She said I was right. Then I said 'Napoleon Hill' and she said, 'Absolutely.' It's an interesting story. She had the benefit of working in the hospital with about 1,100 women, and she's been a May Kay representative for a long time. She started another goal: within six more months she's going to quit physical therapy and sell Mary Kay full time. That's how well she is doing selling the products. This woman certainly had been exposed to Napoleon Hill.

Defining success needs a goal—you need a clear idea in mind, but you have to discipline yourself. I think that happiness defines how successful you are. I'm a father, I've got two kids, and I'm happy. Being in medicine and the military are just chapters in my life. There's an elementary schoolteacher who just recently passed away of cancer, and you couldn't imagine the traffic at her funeral. I don't think you could measure that kind of success, and I certainly know that you cannot measure success in monetary goods.

CHAPTER 7

Applying Napoleon Hill's Principles in Your Own Life

What the mind of man can conceive, it can achieve.

—NAPOLEON HILL

All of the people in this book are considered successful but they followed different paths to define and achieve success for themselves. Some followed the path of education, while others followed the path of perseverance. Some invested their money wisely, while others were meticulous about investing time.

The point is that they all began their journeys with a goal and the desire to achieve that goal. No matter where you live, how much money you have, or the level of education you have attained, your starting point begins with discovering a goal and desire.

Sometimes, the goal and desire will find *you.*

ALVIN YORK and NAPOLEON HILL:
Two Appalachian Success Stories

When I was in my teens, my dad encouraged me to watch the movie *Sergeant York*. At that age, I wasn't interested in a black and white war movie starring Gary Cooper made in the early 1900's. Then, I learned that Alvin York had grown up in The Valley of the Three Forks of the Wolf near Knoxville, Tennessee, just a few hours from our home.

I gave his story a chance to inspire me, and it still inspires me today.

They were worlds apart in many ways, yet Alvin York and Napoleon Hill had much in common. Like Hill, York was born into a family in the central Appalachians in the 1880's. Like Hill, his family survived on hard work and a disciplined lifestyle with little opportunity for formal education. Like Hill, York lost a parent at a young age and was known as an unruly boy who needed guidance.

Their stories diverge with Hill seeking success in the business world and York finding and committing his life to his religious faith before he becomes a war hero. Their lives began to parallel again as both men became embroiled in World War I.

An Attractive Personality . . .

As the war began its destructive sweep across Europe, Alvin York was building Sunday Schools across Fentress County, Tennessee, following a religious conversion that "represented an attempt to master himself [by making] . . . a complete break with his past," a past that was full of rabblerousing, drunkenness, and violence.* The war was still thousands of miles away, appearing in newspapers that were weeks old by the time they arrived in his hollow. Like many in his community, he was patriotic but wanted to avoid violence, which went against the teachings of the Bible. The draft notice that arrived in June, 1917 would force him to resolve that internal battle.

Meanwhile, Napoleon Hill was living in Chicago, where he founded the George Washington Institute, a correspondence course in salesmanship. Living in a large city and surrounded by daily newspapers and radio reports that screamed headlines about the war, Hill would have felt awash in the "apocalyptic tide of history" that seemed to be taking place.† Spurred by his own patriotism, he contacted President Woodrow Wilson to ask what he could do for the war effort. Wilson gave him a job as a propaganda writer, which Hill took without pay. Hill wrote:

> . . . Those who live by the sword die by the sword . . . Sometimes it requires the shedding of much blood and devastation of great fortune to impress this truth upon those who deny it but in the end, the truth still prevails!‡

While Hill was writing these words, York (who had a third grade education) was writing "Don't want to fight" on his appeal for a draft exemption as he struggled with "lingering doubts about the morality of war."§ However, his appeals

---

* David D. Lee. *Sergeant York: An American Hero.* The University Press of Kentucky, 1985.
† Michael Ritt, Jr. & Kirk Landers. *A Lifetime of Riches.* Dutton, 1995.
‡ p. 52–53
§ Lee, p. 17–19.

were denied, so after consulting with his pastor he submitted to his induction into the army.

York's company commander, Major George Edward Buxton, was instantly impressed by York, and also recognized his inner turmoil regarding his objections to war. They spent a great deal of time discussing scriptural references to violence, leaving York with more questions than answers. Buxton did something surprising which attests to the fact that he was so taken with York's character: he gave York a ten-day pass to return to the mountains and think about his offer of a non-combat assignment.

Applied Faith . . .

Like Hill, York had been given the opportunity to work for the war effort without actually participating in the violence, but unlike Hill, York had neither a wife nor children. He secluded himself in the mountains, away from friends and family, and prayed for guidance. He experienced "a second conversion," on that mountain, and returned to the military firmly committed to fighting in the war while keeping Jesus' words "Blessed are the peacemakers . . . " close to his heart.* He told friends and family as he left that God would bring him home alive.

Going the Extra Mile

On October 8, 1918, York was positioned in the Argonne Forest—a dense, thick forest much like the one where he had grown up in Tennessee—where the Germans had created a stronghold. His platoon was ordered to take a railroad that

---

* Lee, p. 22

was held by German machine-gunners. When the Germans returned heavy fire, York and his men were ordered to surround them and most of the men were killed in the gunfire that followed.

The Law of Cosmic Habitforce

Like many of the men who were suffering from the shock of war and low morale, York could have surrendered to the gunfire or to the enemy in the face of what seemed like an unwinnable situation; instead, he chose to recall his method of shooting wild turkeys back in the Tennessee mountains as the best way to deal with the Germans who were advancing toward him as his comrades fell. He began shooting toward the back, so the leaders would not see those falling behind them and drop to the ground, giving them the perfect angle from which to kill York. An excellent marksman, York was able to not only hold off the advancing German column with a pistol, but also silenced the 35 machine gunners that were mowing down Allied soldiers. When York picked up a rifle and demanded surrender, German soldiers began to lay down their weapons one by one. York was credited with capturing 132 prisoners, whom he and the seven able-bodied soldiers marched out of the Argonne Forest. York believed his survival to be "a vindication of his faith."*

When York picked up a rifle and demanded surrender, German soldiers began to lay down their weapons one by one.

---

* Lee, p. 47

Definiteness of Purpose

Napoleon Hill was with President Wilson in early November, 1918 when the Germans requested an armistice.* The President asked for Hill's advice throughout the exchange. On Armistice Day, Hill returned to his office and watched a celebratory parade from his window, wondering what his next step would be. He sat down to write about the war's end and let his pen take over. The result would be a published magazine about Hill's philosophy of success, inspired by the idealism of the Golden Rule.†

In December, 1918, York—a mountain boy who had become an overnight international hero—would also meet President Wilson. He met the President in Paris, the first of many cities to which York would be ushered for awards and honorary tours. In New York, he was met with a ticker-tape parade in his honor. His story was chronicled in the pages of the *Saturday Evening Post* and countless newspapers and magazines.‡

Defining Success

York was offered between $250,000 and $500,000 in deals and endorsements from publications, film companies, and businesses wanting to use his name. Most men, after surviving an ordeal such as York's, would have believed themselves more than deserving of these offers. Certainly, the wealth that fol-

---

* Ritt, Jr. & Landers, p. 57–78.

† p. 60.

‡ Lee, p. 54.

lows such service would have been justified. But York was not the typical man, nor had he entered into military service with the idea of being paid, just as Hill had refused payment for writing about the war. Being paid for endorsing products York didn't use insulted his honesty, and he "felt that commercializing his fame would compromise the high ideals he believed the war was fought to attain."* York refused the offers because he planned to return to his mountain home, where he had no use for fame or wealth. His story would later be immortalized in the movie *Sergeant York*, starring Gary Cooper. He used his revenue from the film to develop more educational opportunities for the people of Tennessee and traveled at his own expense to raise money for education and war-related charities.

It is unlikely that Hill and York crossed paths or that York would have even heard of Hill at that time, but Hill would certainly have read about and heard of Sergeant Alvin York. Hill probably recognized the idealism and old-fashioned values that York embodied, understanding why America wanted him for their hero. Hill might have been reminded of the rural home he left so many years before, and remembered both the poverty and pride of the people there. He might have seen that Alvin York was appealing to the masses because he was Everyman, not a sophisticated, well-educated soldier born and bred in the best of circumstances.

Napoleon Hill might have been surprised to find that York declined nearly half a million dollars, but impressed to know that York took up his calling to public service once again, com-

----

* Lee, p. 63.

mitted to "improving conditions here in the mountains."* It was World War I that led both men to turning points in their lives, where they began to define success in their own ways and found a definiteness of purpose. Perhaps Hill had York in mind as he wrote this passage in preparation for publishing *Hill's Golden Rule*: You can get along with little schooling, you can get along with but little capital; and you can overcome almost any obstacle if you are honestly and earnestly willing to do the best work you are capable of, regardless of the amount of money you receive for it.†

- **Darrell "Shifty" Powers:** A Clinchco, Virginia native, Darrell "Shifty" Powers made history when he parachuted into German-occupied France on June 6, 1944: D-Day, and then served with his comrades in Easy Company in the Battle of the Bulge six months later. A sharpshooter, he won two bronze stars, among several other awards. Following his military duty, he worked for Clinchfield Coal Company for 33 years. He and the 101st Airborne were featured first in the acclaimed book and then HBO film titled *Band of Brothers.*

- **Francis Gary Powers** was born in Jenkins, Kentucky and raised in Pound, Virginia. After graduating from Milligan College in eastern Tennessee, Powers was commissioned in the United States Air Force in 1950. He was assigned to operations in the Korean War, but was recruited by the CIA because of his outstanding record in single engine jet aircraft. By 1960, the 31-year old Pow-

---

* Lee, p. 70.

† Ritt, Jr. & Landers, p. 61.

ers was already a veteran of several covert aerial reconnaissance missions. He left the Air Force with the rank of captain in 1956, to join the CIA U-2 program. Powers' U-2 was shot down by an S-75 Dvina missile on May 1, 1960, over Sverdlovsk. Powers was convicted of espionage against the Soviet Union and sentenced to a total of 10 years in prison, three years of imprisonment followed by seven years of hard labor. The capture was an international incident and was featured in media across the world. However, on February 10, 1962, twenty-one months after his capture, he was exchanged in a spy swap for Soviet KGB Colonel Vilyam Fisher (aka Rudolf Abel) at the Glienicke Bridge in Berlin, Germany. After being debriefed extensively by the CIA, Lockheed, and the USAF on March 6, 1962, he appeared before a Senate Armed Services Select Committee hearing chaired by Senator Richard Russell and including Senators Prescott Bush and Barry Goldwater, Sr. During the proceeding it was determined that Powers followed orders, did not divulge any critical information to the Soviets, and conducted himself "as a fine young man under dangerous circumstances." After his return, Powers worked for Lockheed as a test pilot from 1963 to 1970. In 1970, he co-wrote a book called *Operation Overflight: A Memoir of the U-2 Incident.*

WRITING YOUR OWN
SUCCESS STORY

No matter what your age or circumstances, you can write your story of success just like the people in these pages. Napoleon Hill discovered that he would publish *Hill's Golden Rule* simply by sitting down to write, "The war is over!"*

You can begin with a sentence just that simple.

Start with *your* definition of success. How do you define it? What do you count among your greatest accomplishments? What obstacles did you overcome to reach them?

Draw a timeline, much like the one you see in history books, and illustrate the story of your life in five-year increments. Note what you jot down as your most valuable memories, times of defeat, turning points, and new chapters. Set goals for what you want to see on that timeline in the next five years.

Remember that success comes in many different forms. It is up to you to determine your purpose, your burning desire,

---

* Ritt, Jr. & Landers, p. 58.

and the steps you want to take as your path guides you toward your destiny. You will find some questions in the back of this book that guided the stories of those in these pages.

Now, write your own success story.

Then, make it happen.

Questions to Inspire Your Success Story

1. How do you define success?

2. When you reflect on your life, what do you want to count among your greatest accomplishments?

3. What obstacles, if any, will be presented by your region, gender, ethnicity, age, class or other trait(s)? How will you manage them?

4. What is your burning desire?

5. What is your plan for following your dreams once you determine your purpose? What motivates you to action once you have an idea?

6. Who will be the people allied with you in helping you to become successful? How will you cultivate relationships that will enable you to achieve your goals?

7. Napoleon Hill lists a pleasing personality as having an awareness of 25 different qualities. Of these traits, which do you believe are the most significant in achieving success and why?

- a positive mental attitude
- flexibility
- sincerity
- promptness
- courtesy
- tact
- tone of voice
- habit of smiling
- facial expression
- tolerance
- frankness of manner and speech
- sense of humor
- faith, sense of justice
- appropriate use of words
- effective speech
- emotional control
- alertness of interest
- versatility
- fondness for people
- humility
- effective showmanship
- clean sportsmanship
- a good handshake
- personal magnetism

8. Hill defines faith as "a state of mind through which your aims, desires, plans, and purposes be translated into their physical or financial equivalent . . . the art of believing by doing." In what ways can you use the power of faith to achieve success?

9. In what ways have you "gone the extra mile" or gone above and beyond what was expected of you in your journey toward success? How might you do that as you look ahead to achieving your goals?

10. How do you maintain a positive mental attitude or the "I can . . ." attitude in the face of challenging circumstances? Can you think of a time when a PMA made a difference for you?

11. What techniques do you use to stay focused on your goals, without letting bad habits or distractions get in the way?

12. What is your method for reasoning through a decision or a problem?

13. Describe a time when you learned a valuable lesson from adversity or defeat. How can that lesson inspire you as you move forward?

14. What do you do to get inspired, to cultivate ideas or creativity?

15. Is your health an important factor in your success? What are your habits for maintaining mental/physical health?

16. What is your best technique for budgeting time and/or money?

17. Perhaps the most significant of Hill's principles, this law states that, "every living creature, every particle of matter, is subject to the influence of its environment." But while our environments influence our patterns, they do not dictate our decisions. In what ways will you:
    A. Use your environment as a motivating factor to achieve success?
    B. Overcome your environment to achieve success?
    C. Improve on your environment as you achieved success?

Printed in the USA
CPSIA information can be obtained
at www.ICGtesting.com
JSHW012034140824
68134JS00033B/3045

9 781722 501051